In the Breaking of the Bread

In the Breaking of the Bread

*A User's Guide to a Service of Holy Communion
in the Anglican Tradition*

LEANDER S. HARDING

WIPF & STOCK · Eugene, Oregon

IN THE BREAKING OF THE BREAD
A User's Guide to a Service of Holy Communion in the Anglican
Tradition

Wipf & Stock
An Imprint of Wipf and Stock Publishers
199 W. 8th Ave., Suite 3
Eugene, OR 97401
www.wipfandstock.com

ISBN 13: 978-1-60899-822-7

Manufactured in the U.S.A.

The Rev. Leander S. Harding, Ph.D., is an Episcopal priest who has
served rural, suburban, and urban parishes, and now teaches pastoral
theology at Trinity School for Ministry, Ambridge PA.

For Claudia

"And it came to pass, as he sat at meat with them,
he took bread, and blessed it, and brake, and gave to them.
And their eyes were opened, and they knew him;
and he vanished out of their sight.

And they said one to another, Did not our heart burn within
us, while he talked with us by the way, and while he opened to
us the scriptures? And they rose up the same hour, and returned
to Jerusalem, and found the eleven gathered together, and them
that were with them, Saying, The Lord is risen indeed, and hath
appeared to Simon.

And they told what things were done in the way,
and how he was known of them in breaking of bread.
And as they thus spake, Jesus himself stood in the midst of them,
and saith unto them, Peace be unto you."

—LUKE 24:30–36
AUTH. (KING JAMES) VERSION

Contents

Preface ix
Introduction: The Map xi

1   Thanksgiving 1

2   The Word of God 8

3   The Assembly 15

4   Listening 19

5   Responding 30

6   Making Peace 36

7   The Holy Communion 45

8   The Great Thanksgiving 51

9   The Unforgetting 59

10   The Our Father 72

11   The Breaking of the Bread 77

12   The Sending 88

Preface

THIS LITTLE book has been more than ten years in the making. It started as notes for parish education classes for people who were new to a tradition of Christian worship centered on the service of Holy Communion, the Eucharist. These chapters represent the efforts of one parish priest to explain as simply and straightforwardly as possible what happens in a service of Holy Communion, what it means, and how to enter into the service in a meaningful way.

My hope is that people who are encountering Eucharist-centered worship for the first time will be helped to be taken up in wonder, love, and praise, and that people who are familiar with Eucharistic worship will encounter new treasures that have been hiding in plain sight.

The format of the book is a careful exposition of one of the Eucharistic services in the 1979 Book of Common Prayer of the Episcopal Church USA (Church Publishing Inc., New York). This prayer book is the result of the renewal of liturgical studies in the twentieth century. The service is in the Anglican Book of Common Prayer tradition. Christians of other denominations will be able to apply much of what is said to the service of Holy Communion in their own traditions.

I especially hope that this book will be a help and encouragement to those Christians who are drawn to an ancient-evangelical future.

I want to acknowledge the encouragement that I have received to develop this book from the congregations I have served, and from my students and fellow faculty members at Trinity School for Ministry in Ambridge, Pennsylvania. I am especially grateful to Dr. Christopher Wells, editor of *The Living Church*, for publishing excerpts from the work in progress.

Introduction

The Map

IN THE last chapter of the Gospel according to St. Luke, Chapter 24, beginning in the 13th verse, there is one of the most beautiful and haunting recollections of the risen Christ in the entire New Testament. It is the third day since the Crucifixion and two disciples are walking from Jerusalem to a town called Emmaus, about seven miles distant. It is very likely that they were in a state of profound disappointment and confusion. The Lord in whom they had placed so much hope had died the cruel death Rome reserved for criminals and traitors. The fragile movement that had gathered around this Galilean rabbi had collapsed. People either fled the city like our two friends or went to ground like the group around Peter. As these two disciples are walking on their way to Emmaus they are talking about all the things that have happened.

As they are talking a stranger joins them. He asks them what they are talking about. They were stopped in their tracks by this question and looked sad. The Greek says literally that their faces fell. The disciple named Cleopas answered. "Are you the only stranger in Jerusalem that does not know the things that have taken place there in these days?"

"What things?" said the stranger.

"The things about Jesus of Nazareth, who was a prophet mighty in deed and word before God and all the people, and how our chief priests and leaders handed him over to be condemned to death and crucified him. But we had hoped that he was the one to redeem Israel. Yes, and besides all this, it is now the third day since these things took place. Moreover, some women of our group astounded us. They were at the tomb early this morning and when they did not find his body there, they came back and told us that they had indeed seen a vision of angels who said that he was alive. Some of those who were with us went to the tomb and found it just as the women had said; but they did not see him."

Then he said to them, "Oh, how foolish you are, and how slow of heart to believe all that the prophets have declared! Was it not necessary that the Messiah should suffer these things and then enter into his glory?" Then the stranger began to speak to the two disciples about what the Jewish scriptures, Moses and the Prophets, taught about the Messiah, the savior.

As they walked on their way, engrossed in what the stranger was saying, they came to the village. The stranger made as if to go further. They asked him to stay with them, "for evening is at hand." They went in together and he took the bread and blessed it and gave it to them. It was a very normal thing to do. It was the kind of thing done all the time at Jewish tables, and especially when a group of disciples gathered with their rabbi. In that ordinary moment of the breaking of the bread, the eyes of the two disciples were opened and they recognized the Risen Christ and in that same instant he "vanished from their sight." They looked at each other. They had known it all along. "Did not our heart burn within us, while he talked with us by the way, and while he opened to us the scriptures?" The two disciples returned to Jerusalem and found the others who had had their own encounter with the Risen One and heard the proclamation of eleven that the Lord was risen indeed. In answer, Cleopas and his companion told them about how he had been made known to them in the breaking of the bread.

The Eucharist is a journey. It is a journey from the kingdom of death to the Kingdom of God. It is a journey from the time of this world that is ticking away to the time-fullness of the Kingdom. It is a journey from fear and despair to courage and hope. It is a journey from weakness to power, and from power and privilege to weakness and vulnerability. It is a journey to a place where there is forgiveness and repentance and where itineraries are changed. It is a journey where the extraordinary becomes manifest and communicated through the ordinary. It is a journey upon which we become aware that Christ is with us, teaching us and feeding us and sending us. It is a journey that brings us into holy communion with God, with each other and with the whole Creation. On such a journey it is important to have a map, so that we can visualize the whole journey, so we can know what to expect and how to prepare, so we can see how far we have come and how far we have to go.

The story of the two disciples on the road to Emmaus is presented by St. Luke to his church as just such a map. This story contains every part of the Eucharist. The church has gathered in the persons of the disciples. (Isn't it interesting that it is a rather discouraged church.) Remember how

Jesus says "wherever two or three are gathered in my name, there am I in the midst of them" (Matt. 18:20). The first part of the Eucharistic service is there, the service of the Word. As the two disciples walk along the road to Emmaus, Jesus opens the scriptures to them and their "heart burns" within them. This is the part of the Eucharistic service in which the scripture is read and expounded by the priest in such a way that the presence of Christ in and through the scripture is revealed to us and "our heart burns within us" as he talks to us upon the way. Then we come to the Holy Communion itself where we sit with the Lord at the table and remember what he did and said on the night in which he was betrayed. In that act of thanksgiving the risen Lord becomes known to us in the breaking of the bread. There is also the response of the disciples to this encounter with Christ in Word and Table, and that is that they go and tell others that they have been with the risen Christ who has taught and fed them.

In the following pages I want you to come with me as I meditate upon the words and actions of the Holy Eucharist as it is acted out in a typical parish church. As we do this, we will be walking with Cleopas and his friend on the first day of the week the road to Emmaus. My hope is that at the end of this walk through the Eucharist, our eyes will be less holden (as it says in the King James version), and that we will be more able to recognize him who is there in his life-giving word and in the breaking of the bread.

Thanksgiving

THIS GUIDE is based on the 1979 American Book of Common Prayer, which is used in Episcopal churches, Anglican Church of North America churches, and by many congregations of other traditions.

In the Book of Common Prayer (BCP), on page 355 at the top of the page is written The Holy Eucharist: Rite II. "Rite" is a liturgical word for a fixed form. Rite I uses more traditional language, and Rite III provides for a very free-form service. All rites of the Holy Eucharist have the same basic structure. Rite II is used at the main Sunday morning service in many parishes. In what follows we will be working our way methodically through The Holy Eucharist: Rite II. Much of what follows applies equally well to the other rites and even to the Eucharist as it is practiced in other Christian traditions.

The first thing to notice is the title of the service, The Holy Eucharist. Eucharist is a Greek word. It means literally thanksgiving or the act of thanksgiving. The name of the service of worship upon which we are about to enter is then literally the holy thanksgiving. As we go along in the service we will see some things that are very obviously acts of thanksgiving. When the offerings of bread, wine and money are brought to the altar it is obvious that an act of gratitude is taking place. There is a prayer at the heart of the Eucharist called The Great Thanksgiving and in this prayer specific thanks are offered for the specific ways in which God has blessed God's people. What is not so obvious is that the entire act of worship that we call Eucharist is an act of thanksgiving from beginning to end. The reading and proclamation of the Word is every bit as much an act of thanksgiving as the communion of the bread and the wine. The prayer book makes a powerful statement about Christian worship just by the way the title is laid out on the page. It says that the holy thanksgiving, the supreme act of Christian worship, is the Holy Eucharist and that Eucharist consists of both parts of that journey to Emmaus to which I have already referred. Eucharist includes Word and Table. They belong together and are part of one thing. To have Word without Table or Table without Word is to have half a Eucharist.

The point is made even more clearly on some pages of the BCP that are more rarely seen than the first page of the service. Page 315 is the title page that begins the section of the prayer book that contains all the material pertaining to the Eucharist. It reads The Holy Eucharist in bold type, and below in regular type by way of explanation, The Liturgy for the Proclamation of the Word of God and Celebration of the Holy Communion. Liturgy is an English form of a Greek word that means literally "the work of the people." So here we have a plan for the holy work to which the people of God are called, and that is the proclamation of the Word of God and the celebration of Holy Communion. Through Christ, the eternal Son of God, we have a new and holy communion with God, with each other, and with the whole

Creation. We are called to proclaim and celebrate this new reality through reading and meditating on the scripture and through fulfilling the command given by Jesus on the night in which he was betrayed, "Do this in remembrance of me" (Luke 22:19).

There is another page in the prayer book that is never used in the course of a service but which says a great deal about how Christian worship is understood in the Anglican tradition. On page 13 under the heading, Concerning the Service of the Church, the first sentence of the first paragraph reads, "The Holy Eucharist, the principal act of Christian worship on the Lord's Day and other major Feasts, and Daily Morning and Evening Prayer, as set forth in this Book, are the regular services appointed for public worship in this Church." This is a change for many Episcopalians and for others brought up in Protestant traditions in which the Sunday morning worship centered upon a service of Bible reading, preaching and hymnody. Many Episcopalians grew up with Morning Prayer on Sunday Mornings. For such folk the present emphasis of the church on the Eucharist seems like an innovation and an imitation of Roman Catholic worship. It is not really an innovation but rather is a recovery of the most ancient practice of the church. The present Book of Common Prayer is the result of fifty years of growing ecumenical consensus about the nature of worship in the early church. This renaissance of liturgical scholarship gave rise not only to the revision of the Book of Common Prayer but also to revisions of the Roman Catholic rite, and to the recognition by many Protestant churches that their worship neglects the sacraments in general and the Eucharist in particular. The revised Roman Catholic rite has put more emphasis on the reading of scripture and preaching, and contemporary Protestant worship is recovering the regular celebration of the Eucharist. When the current 1979 Book of Common Prayer was published, it was on the forefront of an ecumenical movement of liturgical reform that recognized that a balanced celebration of Word and Table should be the norm for Sunday morning worship.

Virtually all of the leaders of the Protestant Reformation (16th century) believed from their study of scripture and the history of the Early Church that scripture and preaching in the context of the Lord's Supper was the appropriate service for the celebration of the Lord's Day. They believed that the medieval Mass needed to be cleaned up and purged of the liturgical barnacles that it had acquired in its trip through history. They were also concerned to remove from the Eucharist anything that implied that the liturgy was a ceremony which in some way earned God's forgiveness and love. (A central theme of the Reformation was an insistence on the free gift of forgiveness provided once and for all in the sacrifice of Christ upon the cross. Hence the motto, salvation by grace through faith.)

The first Book of Common Prayer was the result of such reform and revision. Thomas Cranmer (1489–1556), its primary author, was of all the Reformers a man of rare liturgical genius. He translated the existing Latin Mass (communion service) of Salisbury Cathedral in the light of the liturgical revisions of Martin Luther (1483–1546), John Calvin (1509–1564), Martin Bucer (1491–1551), and other Reformers into elegant and poetic English prose. The vision of that prayer book was consistent with the hopes of the Continental (European) Reformers for a church life that would include daily prayer and scripture reading crowned by a service of preaching and the Lord's Supper on Sunday. Unfortunately, the piety of many people during the pre-Reformation period so stressed the unworthiness of sinful people to participate in the Holy Communion that attendance at Mass without eating and drinking the sacred elements had become the norm. Many people went to Mass to witness the miracle of the transformation of the elements into the Body and Blood of Christ. The Reformers rightly felt that this was an attitude that bordered on the superstitious. To combat this mentality, the celebration of the Eucharist without the congregation eating and drinking the elements was forbidden. The Reformers wanted to return the faithful to the piety of the Early Church where the Eucharist was an act of worship by the whole church, whereby the church celebrated its identity as the Body of Christ and its union with the crucified and risen Lord. (In Anglican churches, unlike the Roman Catholic Church, at least one person other than the celebrant must be present in order to celebrate the Eucharist. This is a reminder of the Reformed understanding of the Eucharist that is part of the heritage of our church.) However, because so few people felt worthy to come to the Holy Communion, this rule of the Reformers, which was intended to promote more frequent and meaningful communion, had the opposite effect. The celebration of Holy Communion became less and less frequent until the non-communication which the Reformers abhorred became the norm. From the standpoint of the last one hundred years, the increased emphasis on the Eucharist in the 1979 Book of Common Prayer is an innovation. From the standpoint of the whole of the history of Christian worship, the Sunday morning service of scripture and preaching without the Lord's Supper is an historical accident.

In the United States, the service of Morning Prayer became especially well established because of the shortage of priests in the early days of the Episcopal Church. Until after the Revolutionary War there were no bishops on this side of the ocean; men had to make the dangerous voyage to England for ordination. As a result, many parishes saw a priest just several times a year, and the infrequent celebration of communion became an entrenched tradition.

This quick historical overview may help people raised on Morning Prayer understand the theological and liturgical logic behind insisting on the Holy Eucharist as the primary act of Christian worship, but it will probably not help them with the emotional difficulties that a change of services provokes. The worship experience that we have as children and young people growing up in the church is deeply formative. In some ways, the worship of our childhood years is always the way it should be. Sung Morning Prayer is a very beautiful, inspiring, and uplifting service. It is eucharistic in its own way. The Canticles of Morning Prayer are hymns of praise to the God of creation. By comparison, the service of the Holy Eucharist can seem somewhat solemn and somber. A carelessly said service of Holy Eucharist comes off very badly in comparison to a well-done sung Morning Prayer. All of this I am sure feels like salt in the wound to someone whose childhood convinces them that Morning Prayer is normal and that all of this modern preoccupation with the Eucharist is an aberration. Perhaps this is a problem that only God can fix. I hope that this problem can be at least somewhat helped by a little book like this. For I am convinced that one of the problems that the church faces as it reclaims the way of worship of the New Testament and the ancient Church is that the celebration of the Eucharist requires a greater degree of understanding on the part of the participant. (Especially for adults; children seem to have a natural intuitive way of relating to the Eucharist.) One of the problems may be that we have made a shift in our practice of worship for the best of reasons without in some cases the formation or information that would enable worshipers to gain the full blessing that might be theirs from the recovery of the Eucharist. For many people the Eucharist is like the first part of that journey toward Emmaus. They are walking in disappointment, not yet realizing who it is that walks with them. My hope is that as we work carefully through the service, our eyes will be opened and we will be present at that incredibly sweet moment when the bread is broken in that house in Emmaus.

2

The Word of God

THE NEXT heading that appears on page 355 in the prayer book is The Word of God. If you leaf through the entire service, you will see that this size type is used again on page 361 for the words The Holy Communion. Again by the typography of the prayer book the typology of the service is made clear. So here we begin the service of the Word, the first of the two equal and indispensable parts of the service.

As we go through the service we will see that the liturgy is dense with symbols. Over and over we will come across words that evoke more than one passage of scripture, more than one moment in the history of salvation, more than one theological theme. It is as we begin to hear this rich harmony and become aware of this rich texture that we appreciate what a thing of inexhaustible beauty and meaning the liturgy is. I have already alluded to the way in which the Eucharistic service evokes the story of Emmaus and vice versa. In this first part of the service there is another biblical location that comes to mind. It is also recorded in the Gospel according to St. Luke, in the 4th Chapter, beginning with verse 14. Jesus has just begun his ministry after being tested in the desert. He begins to preach in Galilee and to teach in the synagogues. One Sabbath he goes into the synagogue in his hometown of Nazareth and, "He stood up to read, and the scroll of the prophet Isaiah was given to him. He unrolled the scroll and found the place where it was written, 'The Spirit of the Lord is upon me, because he has anointed me to bring good news to the poor. He has sent me to heal the brokenhearted, to proclaim release to the captives and recovery of sight to the blind, to let the oppressed go free, to proclaim the year of the Lord's favor.' And he rolled up the scroll, gave it back to the attendant and sat down. The eyes of all in the synagogue were fixed upon him. Then he began to say to them, 'Today this scripture has been fulfilled in your hearing.'" In the first part of the service of the Holy Eucharist we are with Jesus in the synagogue as he reads these words from the prophet Isaiah and startles the people present with the incredible assertion that these words have come true in their hearing—in our hearing.

Notice how Christian worship incorporates the worship of the synagogue. It was the custom of the people of Israel to come together on the Sabbath to read the Word of God, to ponder the Torah, the Way, as the five books of Moses were called. The heart of the Torah is the Ten Commandments. On the Sabbath the Jewish people would hear again the Torah that was given to them by God through the prophet Moses in order that they might live always as free people and not fall back into slavery (Exod. 32:15–16, Deut. 10:1–5). They would read the story of the history of Israel and of how God over and over guided, protected and saved God's people. They would also read the prophets. The ministry of the prophets was to recall the people of Israel to the Torah when they departed from it, as they often did, whoring after false gods and becoming immersed in immorality and impiety. This reading of the Hebrew scriptures, what we call the Old Testament, with commentary by elders and teachers, was the standard Sabbath worship in the Jewish synagogue.

The portion of scripture that Jesus reads on that Sabbath morning at the beginning of his ministry is of special interest to us as we try to understand what we are doing at this point in the Eucharist. This portion of the prophet Isaiah was written almost six hundred years before the birth of Jesus. It is from the time of the Babylonian exile. Jerusalem and the Jewish kingdom had been conquered by the Babylonian empire under King Nebuchadnezzar (605–562 BC). The walls of the city were broken down and the Temple, the heart of Jewish religion and worship, was destroyed and defiled. In order to keep the region from becoming a threat again, its inhabitants were forcibly relocated to Babylon. This kind of forced resettlement is a favorite tactic of harsh and nervous victors. Our own government practiced it against American Indians, and Hitler, Stalin, and the Khmer Rouge have all found it useful. It is a devastating experience for the vanquished. We might think of American Indians struggling to retain their dignity and culture in urban centers to give us a clue about what it was like for the people of Israel. Psalm 137 gives us some insight into this moment. Apparently the Babylonians asked the poets and musicians of the Hebrew court to sing some of the famous songs of Zion (Jerusalem). It was the same sort of unthinking cruelty that asks American Indians to perform sacred dances for the entertainment of tourists. The

Psalmist says that they answered by hanging their harps in the trees by the banks of the river of Babylon. "For how could we sing the Lord's song in a strange land?"(Ps 137:4)

After they had been there almost three generations, there arose a prophet called Isaiah. This prophet promised that a Messiah, a Savior, an anointed one, was coming. Messiah means anointed one and Christ is the Greek word for Messiah. This leader, anointed like the Kings of old with the Holy Spirit of God, would lead the people back to the holy city of Jerusalem and restore the Temple and the fortunes of Zion. Isaiah is proclaiming to the captives in Babylon that the Savior is coming to set them free from their bondage and return them from their exile. The new and restored Kingdom will truly be the Kingdom of God where the Torah is truly kept. This new Kingdom will be a Kingdom of Shalom—of peace. Shalom means not only the absence of violence and oppression but also the satisfaction of every spiritual and physical need. The time of the Messiah and the Kingdom of God will be a time of healing, of sight to the blind, of the lame walking, of the poor being fed. It will be a time when men and women are restored to right relation with God and with each other. In their exile and captivity, six hundred years before Christ, the prophet Isaiah consoled the people of Israel with the promise that this King and this Kingdom would soon come. They were not to lose heart. They were not to forget the Torah. They were not to become easy in Babylon. They were to get ready to go home, to leave this alien land and to return to their true abode where they could rightly worship God and live in the way God intended for them to live, enjoying the blessings reserved for God's people.

This prophecy was at least partially fulfilled for the people of Israel. In about the year 580 BC, after Babylon had been conquered by the Persian Cyrus, the people of Israel were allowed to return. Under Nehemiah and Ezra, the Temple was rebuilt and the kingdom was restored. You can read about this in 2 Chronicles and in the books of Ezra and Nehemiah. The restored kingdom never reached the physical splendor or the moral and religious vitality of the prophet's vision. Subsequent kings proved to be increasingly corrupt and disappointing; the people of Israel longed for the coming of the true Messiah. John the Baptist very purposefully evoked the words of Isaiah in his ministry, warning people to get ready for the coming of the Messiah. At the time of Jesus the people of Israel had been conquered many times since the restoration of the Temple, first by Alexander's Greek empire (356–323 BC), and most recently by the Romans. Their existence was very much like the existence of the people of Eastern Europe before the collapse of communism. They lived as vanquished and humiliated people under foreign occupation with foreign troops stationed on their soil, their economy depressed and impoverished by the taxes and trade policies that favored the victor nation. It was especially galling for the Jews that the victors were idolaters and polytheists. The pious Jews of this time longed with all their being for the Messiah, for liberation, for the renewal of the Kingdom. Some of them realized that the Messiah and the Kingdom of which Isaiah spoke could not be brought about by purely political means—it must be an act of God, even a supernatural act. Some thought the Messiah, the Son of Man, would come on the clouds with an army of angels to judge the wicked, redeem the righteous, and establish the Kingdom.

Against this background you can see what an incredible thing it is that Jesus says "Today this scripture has been fulfilled in your hearing." It is at one and the same time incredible good news, unbelievable, and an offensive blasphemy that toys with the hopes of desperate people.

Both the church as a corporate reality and the individual believer must in their development retrace the history of Israel, of the people of God. Now as we begin the Eucharist, we are like the people of Israel in the time of Jesus, and that time was like the exile in Babylon. The world we live in is a world where God is mocked and where the Torah is forgotten. It is easy to be at ease in Babylon and to forget our identity as God's people, as people of the Way. It is easy to be overwhelmed by the evil and corruption. It is easy to forget the songs of Zion, to forget how to worship, to forget even that we were made for worship. Yet we know that things are not as they ought to be. We know that our relationship with God is not as it ought to be, and that our relationship with our fellow human beings is not as it ought to be. Increasingly we are becoming aware that our relationship with the rest of God's Creation is not as it ought to be. In this bondage and exile we remember the prophets, we remember the deliverance of old, and we long for the perfect fulfillment of Isaiah's promise, and we listen with astonishment to Jesus as he says, "Today this scripture is fulfilled in your hearing." Today God has acted for our redemption and sent us his Messiah, the Christ.

Now obviously the world has not been completely remade. Christians believe that in Jesus the Kingdom has been initiated, and through his death and resurrection and the coming of his Spirit the church is called and empowered to witness to the Kingdom, which will come in perfection with Christ at the end of time. The life of the church, especially its worship and especially the Eucharist, is a foretaste of the Kingdom. As we enter the time of worship, we leave the time of the world, the time of *chronos*, the time of ticking clocks, and we enter the time of God, the time of *kairos*, the time of the Kingdom and of the Messiah. The Eucharist is a witness to us of the important truth that ordinary time can become the time of the Kingdom and that bread and wine can communicate to us the very life of God. The Eucharist celebrates the transformation of this ordinary life, this fallen and sinful world into that extraordinary life and sacred world for which we were made. All of this is in the background as we enter upon the Service of the Word and enter into the travail, hope and deliverance of Israel.

3

The Assembly

LET US imagine now the beginning of the Sunday morning Eucharist in a local parish church. The liturgy really begins before the first hymn is played or the altar party
makes its procession through the church and the ministers
take their place. The Eucharist begins as people make their
way from their homes to the church building to bear witness to their identity as the church, the *ekklesia*, those called
out to be the Body of Christ and say with him, "Today this
scripture is fulfilled in your hearing"(Luke 4:21 NIV), to join
in his offering of his life to the Father, and to be renewed in
his new and risen life.

It is very important for Christian people to understand that they do not go to church to attend the services as
a theater-goer goes to the theater to be entertained by the
show. You do not go to church. You are the church. St. Paul
says, "You are the body of Christ and individually members
of it"(1 Cor. 12:27 RSV). St. Augustine says to his people,
"Become this mystery that you touch"(the Body of Christ).
The Eucharist is an act by the whole church. Each member
of the Body has a role to play. Some of this is obvious as
in the altar guild or the choir, the lectors and the acolytes,
who spend many unseen hours each week preparing for

the celebration on Sunday morning. It is easy to see that the service would be nearly impossible without their special work. What is not as obvious is that the liturgy would be impossible without the assembly of the people. The Eucharist is corporate prayer or common prayer par excellence. It is of necessity prayer offered by a body of people, a body of people who are called to be the Body of Christ, and in the Eucharist remember and reconstitute this fundamental identity that they were given in baptism. When people say that they didn't get much out of the service, it may be a judgment on the ministry of the presider or the preacher but it certainly reveals a very impoverished understanding of what this primary act of Christian worship is all about. You come to the Eucharist not so much to get something as to offer something and to become something. It has been said that most people think of worship as though it were the theater. They think that the primary actor is the preacher, the prompter is the Holy Spirit, and the congregation is the audience. In reality, it is the priest who is the prompter and the congregation who is the main actor and God Almighty who is the audience.

If we could regain this sense of what we are about when we gather for worship it would drastically change what we in fact get out of the worship service. We would come not as a passive audience but would understand ourselves as people who are called into a new society, a new brotherhood and sisterhood, which is called to have a starring role in the drama of God's communication of God's redeeming love to the world. Our society is a society in which there is great loneliness and in which it is difficult for people to have experiences of community and solidarity. Many contemporary people live very isolated lives. The experience of a body of people united in community and engaged in a common act that gives their lives meaning and value is for many people an almost unknown experience. But this is exactly what the Eucharist is, and for that reason it is more important than ever that we understand who we are meant to be as we offer the Holy Sacrifice in, with, and through Christ, and that we allow that knowledge to transform our lives together inside and outside the church.

Something else needs to be said about this gathering of the assembly without which the Eucharist is impossible, and that has to do with the fact that God is there ahead of us calling us together. One of the very good things that are happening in all Christian churches today is the rediscovery of the power of the Holy Spirit in the renewal movements. People are talking about the power of God's Holy Spirit and witnessing to the power of this Spirit moving in their lives. I believe that sometimes there is an unintentional negative side effect to some of this talk, and that is that the casual listener may be misled and begin to think that the Holy Spirit of God is to be found primarily in profound and vivid religious experiences. I don't want to downplay the significance of such experiences. But I don't want us to miss the more quiet and ordinary work of God's Holy Spirit in the heart and mind of every Christian person. When you get out of bed on Sunday morning and make your way to the church you are responding to inspiration, the in-breathing of God's Holy Spirit, and you are responding to the call of God to come closer to God and to know God better. That call of God calls you into community with others in the fellowship of the Spirit. The fellowship of the Holy Spirit is another name for the Body of Christ, the Church. To see a parish assemble for worship on Sunday morning is to see God at work in God's people as the Holy Spirit, leading, guiding, gathering. It is a very quiet and much overlooked miracle.

4

Listening

As THE church fills, people prepare themselves for worship in different ways. Often a person, upon entering the pew, will make some gesture of respect toward the altar, in reverence for God. Some people will bow, others will go down upon one knee in what is called a genuflection. Some will at the same time make the sign of the cross. Since customs vary a great deal from parish to parish, and since so many people move many times in their lives, the newcomer is likely to observe a confusing variety of customs and practices, including no observable custom at all. Follow what will help you quiet your own heart. It is important to take a moment of silent prayer to prepare for the worship that is to come. Many people find that gestures such as bowing or genuflecting as a sign of respect, kneeling in prayer as a sign of humility before God, help focus their thoughts and feelings. These customs are not prescribed in the Anglican tradition and sometimes are the cause of unnecessary argument. In all cultures, deep and profound respect expresses itself in posture and gesture. I suspect that the reverse is also true, that certain postures and gestures can help us enter into a worshipful and prayerful attitude.

Typically there is some music before the service begins, the purpose of which is to help prepare the heart and mind for worship. The service often begins with a hymn. In addition to the teaching and inspiration that may be in the hymn, the union of the congregation in song is a demonstration that the community has gathered and is ready to worship God as a body, to engage in the act of common prayer that is the Eucharist.

The people stand and the procession makes its way to the altar. The journey has commenced. We are on our way to Emmaus. We are leaving the kingdom of death and entering the Kingdom of God. We are going to be with Jesus in the synagogue in Nazareth as he proclaims that the Kingdom is present in our midst. We are going to be with him on the night in which he was betrayed. We are going to be present at the Crucifixion. We are going to share the joy and astonishment of the Apostles at the resurrection. We are going to hear the risen Lord give those Apostles a mission and the promise of the Holy Spirit, with power for that mission, and we are going to know that their mission is now our mission.

As soon as the priest has taken his or her place at the altar and the opening hymn has come to a conclusion, the liturgy proper begins on page 355 with an opening acclamation. This is a ritual of recognition. It is very much like the sign and countersign of the soldier on guard duty. In the earliest days of the church when being a Christian was a crime, it was important to have a way of telling who was a Christian. Tracing the sign of the cross with the fingers upon one's head or chest was one such signal of recognition. There also grew up traditional greetings. Instead of saying hello, one would say, "Christ is risen," and another Christian recognizing this would say, "The Lord is risen indeed." This is in fact the opening acclamation used during the Easter season. This opening greeting changes with the season of the year. In addition, there is a special acclamation for the service of Baptism. In the opening acclamation the priest recognizes the congregation as the holy people of God assembled for worship. In this exchange the priest and people greet each other in God's name and in effect say, "We know who we are and why we are here. Let us begin."

In many parishes an unfortunate custom has grown up of the priest beginning the service by greeting the congregation with a hearty "good morning." It is redundant to have two greetings and it is hard to see the point of importing the secular greeting into the liturgy. In the church we have a centuries old way of greeting each other and of recognizing each other as members one of another in the Body of Christ; it is by saying, for instance, "Blessed be God" and answering, "and blessed be his Kingdom now and forever. Amen." The point of the opening acclamation is to call us to the dignity of our identity as God's church and to our vocation of praise and thanksgiving. The acclamation also establishes the rhythm of the dialogue of the liturgy. The celebrant will proclaim the story of God's love made real to us in Jesus Christ and the congregation will acclaim, affirm, and say Amen, May it be so! The dialogue of the liturgy is a dialogue of mutual encouragement in the faith, and it is right that it should begin with a greeting that is profound and dense with meaning.

Sometimes after the opening acclamation, the collect for purity is said (page 355). A collect is a brief prayer that has a particular form. There is a preamble or invocation. God is addressed. There is a meditation. Some attribute or activity of God is described. There is a petition; some particular grace or blessing is asked. The prayer usually ends with a doxology, a sentence of praise to God, Father, Son, and Holy Spirit. The collect for purity is one of the most well-known and beloved in our tradition; it is based on Psalm 51. This prayer recognizes that without the inspiration of God's Holy Spirit we cannot worship God aright and it prays for that grace. It also speaks of the "thoughts of our hearts." The heart in biblical and liturgical tradition is the center of human personality. One sometimes hears the criticism made by opponents of religion that worship is sentimentalism or mere emotionalism. Here at the very beginning of the liturgy is a provision for the inclusion of prayer that asks God to bring emotion and intellect, thoughts, desires, and secrets to the place of worship. In this prayer there is a recognition that true worship is a matter of the human person in wholeness and entirety. It is a prayer that our worship may go beyond sentimentality or mere intellectual exercise, that our worship may be a matter of innermost depths and leave no part of our person uninvolved or untouched.

If you read the italic instructions interspersed in the text of the prayer book, you will see that there are many choices that the celebrant can make as the service progresses. After the collect for purity or immediately after the opening acclamation, if the collect is not used, there is a song of praise, which is sung or said standing, the ancient posture for praise and thanksgiving. In most parishes at the main service on a Sunday morning this part of the service will be sung. There are rich musical settings for the parts of the liturgy that traditionally follow here. The first hymn, on page 356, which begins, "Glory to God in the highest" is in Latin called the *Gloria*. The verses, which are printed side by side in the middle of the page, and which begin "Lord, have mercy" on the left and "*Kyrie eleison*" on the right, are called the *Kyrie*. Below the *Kyrie* is the English translation of an ancient Greek hymn called the *Trisagion*. Some of the greatest music in the Western tradition has been written for these portions of the Eucharist. They have been sung by the congregation from the earliest times. The purpose of these hymns is to allow praise and thanksgiving, awe, wonder, and the desire for love and mercy and blessing to well up in the heart of the worshiper and take root in the gathered congregation. If there is some other more contemporary hymn that may help a particular congregation express its praise, it may be used here. It is important to understand that here the congregation in one voice is addressing God, rejoicing in their knowledge of who God is and asking God to respond to their worship. The liturgy is a conversation; this is a moment when the congregation addresses God in preparation for God's address to them in the reading of and reflection upon the scriptures.

On the top of page 357 in bold type are the words, The Collect of the Day. We have come to another of the moments that make up the service of the word. As noted above, a collect is a short prayer with a particular form. For each Sunday of the Christian year and for many week-days that are set aside to remember a particular figure or event in the Christian life, there is a special collect. Herbert O'Driscoll, the former Warden of the College of Preachers at the National Cathedral, has a wonderful analogy for the collect of the day. He says it is like when you enter a modern shopping mall and approach the map that gives the layout of this vast territory. There is a reassuring red dot that says, "You are here." The collect of the day gives us a particular theme upon which to fix our attention as we listen to the reading of the scriptures. The collect is introduced with a formula that appears over and over, called a salutation. It is another form of greeting, and is often used to quiet a noisy parish hall so that grace can be said before a meal. It is a signal that we are now going to pray and you need to pay attention because at the end of the prayer you will be expected to say Amen, that ancient Hebrew word that means "Let it be so." To say Amen with conviction one needs to hear and understand.

Now come the Lessons. The people sit, which is the traditional posture for learning. One or two lessons may be read. Often a psalm, as the hymns of Israel are called, is sung or said. In the back of the prayer book is printed a lectionary for Sunday morning that is divided into three years, A, B, and C. A lectionary is a system of readings, from the Latin *lectio*. There are appointed readings for every Sunday of the Christian year. The cycle of readings changes on the first Sunday of Advent. If all of the lessons are used, first we will hear a reading from the Old Testament or Hebrew scriptures. We read the Hebrew scriptures because they are the record of God's mighty saving deeds in the past, and because they contain God's self-revelation to the people of Israel, which is still valid for us. We also read of God's promises of salvation and of the sending of a savior, which we believe have come true in Jesus. The church also understands itself as the new Israel and believes that what has happened in the history of Israel will happen over and over in its own life. Both the individual believer and the church as a whole will always find that this story of the people of God on the journey from slavery to freedom and the promised land is also their story. We are also reminded that the story of God's involvement with the human race in Jesus is the latest installment in a very long running serial.

Very often after the first reading, one of the Psalms of Israel is sung or said. The Psalms are the ancient hymnbook of Israel. They have always been at the heart of the prayer of the Christian church. It is said that in the Psalms one can hear Christ praying to the Father and that we can do no better than to pray the prayer that he prayed. The psalms are rich in human emotion and response to God. They contain thanksgiving, praise, awe, wonder—and also doubt, bitterness, and complaint. I am sure to many people they seem arcane. But listen carefully and you will hear the most honest and unvarnished address to God. The Psalms reassure us that there is no emotion that we cannot share with God. It has all been felt before and shared with God before.

The second reading is typically taken from one of the New Testament writings other than the Gospels. Usually it is from one of the letters (epistle is a Greek word for letter) of the Apostles to the struggling churches at the beginning of the Christian era. In these letters the Apostles dealt with fundamental issues of belief and church practice. They constitute a basic clarification of the Gospel and teaching of Jesus by those who had received a special commission for the upbuilding of the church. While these letters are often pertinent to the issues of the individual believer, they are addressed to gathered worshiping communities, to churches, and are best heard that way. As our time begins to resemble more and more the centuries in which the church was founded, their words are powerfully relevant. Sometimes the second reading is taken from the Acts of the Apostles or the Book of Revelation.

At every Eucharist there is always a reading of the Holy Gospel. The word Gospel is an early English form of the words "good news," which is in turn a translation of the Greek word *evangelion*. There are four Gospels: Matthew, Mark, Luke, and John. These Apostles are called the four Evangelists. Each one of the Gospels tells the story of the life of Jesus from the unique perspective of that Gospel writer. Matthew, Mark, and Luke have much material in common. They each give a synopsis of the life of Jesus and are referred to as the Synoptic Gospels. Each year of the Sunday morning lessons focuses on one of these Gospels in turn. The Gospel of John is a more mystical and theological Gospel; each year readings from this Gospel are used during the Easter Season.

The reading of the Gospel is the high point of the first part of the service, the service of the word. There is often some ceremony around the reading of the Gospel. The Gospel is read by one of the ordained ministers called a deacon. Part of the ministry of the deacon is to have a special responsibility for the poor, the sick, and the imprisoned. It is fitting that the words of Jesus, which are good news to the poor and healing to the sick and release to the captives, be read by the deacon. (If a deacon is not present, one of the priests will read the Gospel.) It is important to understand that the good news of the Gospel is addressed to those who are poor in the things of this world and also to us who are spiritually impoverished. It is a word of God's compassion and healing love to those who are sick in body and also to us sick of soul. It is a word of hope to those who languish in prison and to those of us who are imprisoned in bitterness, hopelessness, and despair.

There are often other ceremonies that attend the reading of the Gospel. The prayer book (page 357) instructs the congregation to greet the announcement of the Gospel by standing in respect and with the words, "Glory to you, Lord Christ." After the reading is completed, we acknowledge the reading with the words, "Praise to you, Lord Christ." We believe that in Jesus the eternal word of God's Love has become flesh. We believe that the Holy Scriptures are the progressive revelation of God's word of love addressed to the human race. It is like an artist who in a series of works invests more and more of self in the work until finally a work is created which is a perfect self-expression. God wants us to know God, and has been at work to bring us to the place where we can recognize the Word of God. Finally in the fullness of time, after the preparation of the whole history of the people of Israel, after the prophets, God's Word, which is (because it is God's Word) God himself, comes to perfect expression in the Creation in a person, the person of Jesus Christ. In the Eucharist we are celebrating the transforming presence of God's Word of Love, of Christ, in our midst. This is a word that convicts, challenges, consoles, and transforms us. The congregation greets and acknowledges the Gospel as the sacred presence of Christ in our midst.

Often there is a Gospel procession. The Gospel Book, sometimes clothed in a beautiful cover, is carried with great reverence into the midst of the people. This procession may be accompanied by torches or incense. As the Gospel Book is carried down the aisle, the congregation turns to face it, and the focus is on the Gospel. When the Gospel is announced the reader may lift the book high. This ceremony is like the ceremony that attends the consecration of the bread and wine in the service of the Holy Communion. It is all a way of calling attention to the presence of the Holy One in our midst, to Christ's real and abiding presence in, with, and through the scripture, God's Holy Word.

Sometimes when the Gospel is announced, you may see the faithful trace a small cross on their forehead, lips, and heart as they greet the Gospel. These personal acts of ceremonial and piety are not prescribed in our church, and the custom varies a great deal. This particular custom expresses the desire of those hearing the Gospel that God's word may be in their thoughts, upon their lips, and in their hearts.

Immediately after the reading of the Gospel is the sermon or homily. The people are seated, and the priest has the awesome responsibility of standing in the place of Jesus as he walks on the road to Emmaus with the disciples and opening the scriptures in such a way that "our heart burns within us," as it says in Luke 24:32. The purpose of the sermon is to help the congregation hear the scriptures of the day as God's word addressed to us today. One of the best explanations of the task of the preacher was made by the Rev. Paul Gibson, who was at the time the Liturgical Officer of the Church of Canada. He said that the scripture presents an original Christ event and that Christ is at work today in our world and in our lives, and the job of the preacher is to stand between these two Christ events pointing in both directions, making the connection.

In all but the most unusual circumstances, the sermon follows the lectionary readings very closely. One of the challenges that contemporary preachers face is that the lectionary system, where portions of larger works are read, depends on the idea that the congregation is familiar with the outline of the Bible as a whole and has encountered the Sunday readings before in private reading and study. It is as though the congregation hears four bars of a familiar song, then hears the preacher say, "OK, we all know that song; now . . ."—the problem is we don't all know the song. Developing the practice of reading and reflecting on the scriptures either privately or with a small group of others during the week before the Sunday Eucharist will enrich the worshiper's experience of the Service of the Word.

5

Responding

THE NICENE *Creed*. On Sundays and principal feast days, immediately after the sermon, the congregation rises and recites the Nicene Creed in unison, all standing (page 358). The Nicene Creed is a very ancient summary of Christian belief. Nicaea is the name of an ancient city that was located in what is now Turkey. In 325 AD, the emperor Constantine called a conference of bishops, a council, to settle fundamental disputes about Christian belief. The focus of the council was the understanding of the personhood of Jesus Christ. Was Jesus Christ really God incarnate? Was he a man who had been adopted by God? Was he God only appearing to be human? The unity of the early church, not to mention the unity of the empire, was threatened by the lack of a normative definition of the Christian faith. The Creed that the Council ultimately produced is more of a formula for understanding who Jesus is than an exhaustive definition. The Nicene Creed rejects any definitions of Jesus that compromise either his divinity or his humanity. Only God could save us and only one who truly shared our human condition could save us. Jesus must be truly God and truly human. The Nicene Creed is a very basic outline of Christian faith in God who is Father, Son, and Holy Spirit.

One phrase of the Creed is confusing to many people. "We believe in one holy catholic and apostolic Church." It can sound as though one were being asked to confess belief in the Roman Catholic Church. The word "catholic" means universal. The fathers of the council were simply saying that they believed in that church which has always and everywhere existed since the time of the apostles. The Nicene bishops were affirming their desire to remain connected to the tradition and teaching of the first followers of Jesus, to pass on the faith intact. The Nicene Creed was intended as a summary of the most ancient Christian belief; this phrase was a signal from the members of the council that they did not believe or wish that they were communicating anything which had not always and everywhere been believed. The Nicene Creed is used regularly by the Anglican Communion, the Roman Catholic Church, and most of the Protestant churches. The Creed is the property of the whole church.

The congregation has been sitting for the teaching of the homily or sermon. The scripture has been opened and interpreted, and made a living word for the lives of the listeners as individuals and as a gathered community. The purpose of the sermon was to strengthen the faith, commitment, and understanding of the faithful. Now the people respond, affirming their faith in the words of this ancient Creed, uniting their voices with the voices of generations upon generations of Christians throughout the world in the confession of a common faith. This is the reason why the Creed begins in fidelity to the verb form in the most original text, "We believe." The "We" is not only this particular gathered congregation celebrating this particular Eucharist.

It is also the entire Christian community spread out in time and space.

The Prayers of the People. After the Creed come The Prayers of the People. The people either remain standing or kneel for the prayers, according to the custom of the place. Certain individuals with strongly held preferences for a posture other than the local custom can usually be observed in most of our churches. It is confusing to the newcomer, who is advised to conform to the majority use, but it is also a witness to the diversity and tolerance of our church in matters of nonessentials.

The Prayers of the People are often led by one of the laity or by a deacon as the minister whose special responsibility it is to represent the needs of the world to the church. This is one of the points in the Eucharist when it is most clear that the worship of God is the action of the whole gathered community. It is the gathered church that prays as one for the universal church, for the nation and all in authority, for the welfare of the world, for the concerns of the local community, for all who suffer, and for the departed. There are six forms, beginning on page 383. This is one of those points in the service when persons new to prayer book worship often lose their place in the prayer book. They are going along in great shape following the creed, they turn the page, and suddenly they are on page 359 and the rest of the congregation is thirty pages ahead. It can be even more confusing in those congregations that regularly rotate their usage of the six forms provided. Check the service bulletin at the beginning of the service or place one's self strategically near a more experienced worshiper so that the right page can be quickly cribbed.

During these prayers there are moments of silence when members of the congregation are encouraged to add the names of persons or events with which they are particularly concerned. We are also encouraged to "Thank God for all the blessings of this life." This time of the prayers of the people is rich in those congregations where the people have learned to bring their concerns to the Eucharist and share them during the prayers of the people. All these hopes and fears, petitions and thanksgivings, can then be put on the altar with the bread and wine. Then the elements have a deep and tangible connection with the daily life of the people. In earlier days, when the community had actually to make the bread and wine for the altar, it was perhaps clearer that in the Eucharist we put our ordinary life, our daily bread upon the altar so that united with Christ it could become for us sacramental food, the means by which God shares his very life with us. It helps to make the celebration more vivid when families take turns making bread and providing the wine for the holy meal. But for the Eucharist to express fully the power it can have for us, it is important that we bring our prayers to the assembly, uttered aloud in the face of the congregation, to place them on the altar.

In many congregations the people are quite used to praying aloud for their loved ones, for the poor, for the suffering, and for the peace of the world. It is striking though how often there is a great silence when prayers are invited in thanksgiving for the blessings of this life. Counting blessings is a skill that needs to be practiced, and the lack of practice in public liturgy impoverishes the spiritual life of the entire congregation. In the Eucharist God causes ordinary things, bread and wine, to become the means by which God feeds us with God's very life. God wants all of life to be Eucharist for us. God wants all relationships, all human transactions, all our work, all our interaction with the rest of the Creation to be Eucharist, a partaking of the life of God that causes thanksgiving to well up in us and draw our hearts to God and to a new unity with each other. What we get when we come to the Eucharist is a template, an archetype. We are to go out and apply the template, look for the type of the archetype, and finding the match, return, giving thanks. The celebration of our parish Eucharists would be greatly enriched if each worshiper would come to church prepared to share during the prayers one way in which God had blessed him or her in the week past. This need not be done at the top of one's lungs, but simply loud enough to be heard by those sitting nearby. Certainly if one felt oneself the recipient of a remarkable blessing one would want to share that with the whole congregation. This is also a time when leaders of the congregation, clergy and lay alike, ought to share their celebration of blessings that have come to the congregation as a whole. The simple business of recognizing and counting blessings is indispensable to a right relationship to the celebration of the Eucharist, and to the cultivation of the Eucharistic consciousness in the individual and the congregation that is so fundamental to the Christian life.

Sometimes at the end of the prayers of the people, the celebrant will say a collect that, much to the confusion of the person meticulously following the service in the prayer book, does not appear on the page on which that particular form of the prayers of the people appears. The collect can be taken from those on pages 394 and 395 or may even be another suitable collect. This need not be a cause for panic if you have a general idea where the service is going and what comes next. You can just listen to the collect. Usually at the end of the prayers of the people the worshiper will want to turn back to page 360 for the confession. (The one exception is when form VI is used, which concludes with its own confession.)

6

Making Peace

CONFESSION. THE confession of sin is not always part of the celebration of the Eucharist but usually follows here in the major celebration of the parish on most Sundays. We are coming to the culmination of the Service of the Word. We have heard the Word of God's sacrificial love for us and for the good Creation in the words of scripture. Those words of scripture have been made a living Word to us by the activity of the Holy Spirit in the heart of the preacher and in our hearts as listeners. This receiving of God's Word, which is ritually recognized in the greeting of the Gospel and in saying Amen to the words of the preacher, gives rise naturally to the prayer of the gathered church for the world and for the church in petition, thanksgiving, and confession. Here the structure of the Eucharist as a dialogue, a conversation with God, is very much in evidence. We have heard God's Word of Love addressed to us, and our response includes a renewed conviction of our faith, a renewed earnestness in prayer, and a renewed confession.

Very often parents are shocked when they know their child has committed some offense and the child refuses to confess and own up to the wrongdoing, even when confronted with the evidence. It should not be so surprising, and parents should not insist on a standard that runs so counter to the drift of human nature. When we believe that admitting to wrongdoing will cause us to lose love and to be rejected and abandoned, we are unwilling to confess even when caught red-handed. The human heart is constructed in such a way that the fear of being abandoned and rejected and left utterly loveless will override all else, even the sense of reality and sober self appraisal. Rather than risk the categorization "bad" and the verdict unlovable, the human heart will forget, obscure, re-construe, and qualify with a hundred exonerations any wrongdoing. It is only a profound conviction of an unshakeable love that allows us to admit to ourselves and to God the exact nature of our wrongs. Only after the address to us of God's gracious Word of Love are we able to confess our sins and in the light of that love to look realistically at the character of our relationship with God, with our brothers and sisters, and with the good Creation which God has put into our care. The act of confession, which brings to light those things that we have been trying so mightily to justify and excuse, or which we have been trying so hard not to think of because "the burden of them is intolerable," is an indispensable part of our growing intimacy with God in this conversation of love. You cannot be intimate with someone when you are pretending to be someone that you are not. In the confession we cease to pretend to ourselves, to God, and to each other that we and our world are other than they are. It is a moment of honesty that allows us to grasp in gratitude God's continual forgiveness of us, and that creates in us the desire to amend our lives and our communities. When we confess our sins, we open ourselves to the power of God's love to work in our hearts a transformation that will enable us to live more nearly as God intends human beings to live.

Let us turn to the actual words of the confession as they appear on page 360. We are invited to make our confession with the words, "Let us confess our sins against God and our neighbor." The meaning here is not sins against God and sins against neighbor. The meaning here is that it is impossible to sin against God without sinning against our neighbor and vice versa. When we wrong our neighbor, or any other part of the Creation including ourselves, we wrong the Creator. When we wrong God, we act in a way that makes true human community impossible and that engenders injustice, cruelty and destruction. In this invitation to confession, we are also reminded of the fact of liturgy which is so difficult for contemporary people to comprehend, that when we worship we are individuals, with our more private sense of wrongdoing and alienation from God and other human beings, and we are also a gathered group with a corporate identity. The church is a great democracy of sinners. It is the conviction of the church that each one of its members—bishops, priests, deacons, and laity—each one is always in continual need of confession. The more we bring into the light of God's love, the more we are aware of God's love, the deeper we are able to let the transforming power of God's love take hold in us.

No one comes to the liturgy that week with nothing to confess, for we all share in the human situation which concretely in terms of the life of this particular congregation, and more universally in terms of the state of the world, is not as it should be, not as God intends. In the confession we are called to repent not only for our private acts of violence toward self, toward others, and toward the Creation, which are all in the end different species of the same genus: violence toward God. We are called to repent as a group, as a congregation with a corporate identity, for the way in which our corporate life falls short of God's vision and misses the aim of God's intention. As the church we repent on behalf of humankind. The need for confession will never cease until quite literally Kingdom come, when God and humanity and the Creation are completely and fully in the relation they were intended from all eternity by God to have.

In the prayer of confession, we confess that we have sinned in "thought, word, and deed." Sin is a state of being out of relationship, not having the intimacy with God we were meant to have and therefore being out of right relationship with our brothers and sisters and fellow creatures. The state of being gives rise to thoughts, words, and deeds. In confession we are bringing things to light in the hope of acting in a different way, but we understand that acts flow from being, from a state of character or what the ancients would call a state of soul. The confession recognizes the solidarity of our actions with our speech, thoughts, and innermost disposition.

We sin both by "what we have done and by what we have left undone." Many people take refuge in the assurance that they have done nothing wrong. The new life with God is not only a matter of restraint but also of a passion for acts of love, charity, forgiveness, and justice. This leads us to the confession of the root of all our sins and this is that we "have not loved God with our whole heart." The whole heart is a biblical way of saying with the entire person, the whole being. We have not made God's love for us, and the love of

God in us that answers that love, the center of our identity. All sin is ultimately the love of the wrong thing, or the love of the right thing in the wrong way. We are to love God in and through all things. When we mistake the creature for the Creator, when we try to get from our relationship with another human being or from our work, or from some substance like alcohol or drugs, or even from our relationship with nature, the love, meaning and purpose which we can only get from God, then we are not loving God with our whole heart. When our love is thus distorted, it is inevitable that we will damage ourselves and those communities to which we belong, and we will damage the Creation. Maria Montessori tells the story of a little boy of five years old who comes home from religious instruction and asks his mother, "Mother, who do you love more, God or me?" The mother hastens to reassure the child, "Of course, I love you more." "I thought so," says the child, "and I think that is your problem." Even a child knows that such a lack of perspective can only end in disaster for everyone. We will crush the life out of our loved ones if we turn on them the terrible weight of our need to love and be loved by an infinite love.

"We have not loved our neighbors as ourselves." This is another way of saying that we have not loved God aright. I once had a bishop who was fond of a very simple description of the Christian life. He explained that the Christian life has three variables: love of God, love of neighbor, love of self. The living of the Christian life is simply striving for a more perfect love of these three variables. It does not matter where you start. If you learn to love God better, you will love your neighbor and yourself better and so on right round the clock. You cannot learn to love your neighbor better without coming to a new love of God. And if you learn to love yourself in the right way, that is love yourself with some measure of the love which God has for you and to which the life and death and resurrection of Jesus witness, you must love God and your neighbor more rightly. I would include that to love God, neighbor, and self includes by definition a love of the whole created order. In the confession we are reminded of these interconnections and are invited to the conversion and transformation of our individual and corporate lives to a deeper identification with that one human being who loved God perfectly in all things and through all things, and so turned the face of a perfect love toward his fellow human beings, God's eternal son, Jesus Christ.

As we meditate on the inevitably disordered state of our loves, our distance from God and each other, our abuse of the Creation, our desire for healing and restoration, and on God's gift of love to us and God's desire to reconcile us to each other and to him in Christ, "we are truly sorry and we humbly repent," asking God for the sake of Jesus to have mercy on us. We ask God to forgive us, for the harm we do to ourselves and to each other and to the Creation is harm done to God. The mercy we ask for is that God will give us a change of heart, and we ask that "we may delight in your will, and walk in your ways, to the glory of your Name. Amen."

Absolution. Notice that the rubric provides that the bishop when present gives the absolution (page 360). The bishop is the representative of the Apostles. Jesus gave to the Apostles the task of proclaiming to God's people the good news of God's forgiveness of sins. On most Sundays in most parishes, the bishop is not present, and the priest celebrating the liturgy gives the absolution. The form makes it clear that it is God who does the forgiving but it also makes clear that the church through its ordained ministers is able to forthrightly declare this absolution and forgiveness, which is ours through Christ. The absolution also makes clear that God's forgiving love not only recognizes and loves us in spite of our sins and the injury we do God, but that this forgiving love "strengthens us in all goodness." The prayer ends with a remarkable assertion. The celebrant, who is ordained to speak the Word of love that creates what it proclaims and names, says, "by the power of the Holy Spirit keep you in eternal life." Now here is a remarkable thing. Eternal life, the new life that is the result of the new relationship with God and each other that is ours in Christ, the life that was in Christ, was Christ and which the resurrection shows is a life that the grave cannot hold, is not only something we are meant for and will come to some day on the other side of the Jordan when we are done with this old life. Eternal life is something that is here and now. Even in our imperfection, our missing the mark, our sinfulness, eternal life is something that we have not entirely fallen out of, and in which the power of God's Holy Spirit keeps us. In this old life, the new life has appeared. In time, a life, which in the end time is not big enough to hold, has appeared, and we are given the gift of that life and the power of the Holy Spirit to keep us in it.

At the end of the absolution is an "Amen" in italics. The congregation says amen, let it be so. Let it be so for each one of us and for all of us as a group. Let it be true for the whole human race.

The Peace. The people now rise to their feet and the priest greets them with the words, "The peace of the Lord be always with you." The people reply, "And also with you." People turn and greet their neighbors, saying "God's peace" or "the peace of the Lord," with a handshake or a hug depending on the custom of the congregation. This sometimes becomes an exchange of affection between old friends and the level of physical intimacy including great bear hugs can be off-putting to newer members of the congregation. This is unfortunate because the peace that is being shared here is something other than the ordinary affection that springs up between friends and associates that share a history and common life. The point of this peace is that it is a peace which is not natural but which is the gift of the Spirit of Christ. It may bring you to see friends and family and associates in a new light. When in the exchange of the peace you greet someone that you do not know and with whom you are most unlikely upon any other basis to have even an acquaintance, you are experiencing more of the secret of this part of the liturgy and real meaning of Christ's peace. Jesus has come to bring us into a new relationship with God, and because we are being brought into a new relationship with God we are being brought into a new relationship with our fellow human beings. In this peace the natural divisions of race, class, age, and social status that keep people apart are overcome. Even the categories of righteousness and unrighteousness, of decent and indecent people, are overcome. Congregations that are not constantly adding to their ranks the most unlikely collection of people, including persons who have abandoned lives of obvious immorality for the Christian way of life, are missing some of the power and profundity that is in the exchange of the peace. Here we are a great democracy of sinners, all in need of forgiveness and all freely forgiven, sharing the joy of being undeserving winners in the cosmic lottery of God's love.

7

The Holy Communion

THE OFFERTORY. Now we are in the second part of the service, the Holy Communion. Having heard Jesus as he opened to us the scriptures, we now remember the night in which he was betrayed, and we like the disciples in Emmaus will recognize him as he makes himself known in the breaking of the bread. The offertory is composed of all those actions that represent the offering of the people. This is when the collection is taken up. This is when a special offering of music by the choir or church musicians is made, and this is when the gifts of bread and wine are brought forward from the midst of the congregation and placed upon the altar. Often before the collection is taken or the anthem sung or the elements brought forward, announcements are made. Announcements can be made in several other locations but this is the place where they most often occur in most parish churches. If they go on too long or become merely a community bulletin board they can disrupt the service, but brief announcements at this point that are relevant to the life of the community reflect the real gathering of our lives, the life of the church and the life of the world, into the offering that is being presented to God.

One of the things that sadly and inevitably happen to the sacramental worship of the church over time is the taming of sacramental symbols. Baptism by total immersion becomes a few drops delicately dropped on a baby's head. Oil poured from a beaker over the head for healing becomes a smudge rubbed from a saturated piece of cotton. Thick, crusty, yeasty bread becomes the conventional communion wafer. It is often said about these wafers that it is easier to believe that it is Jesus than that it is bread. Even the bread and wine that we offer are concealed in special containers which make them look otherworldly. In many parishes the offering of money is bagged or otherwise made to look dignified. A great gaudy pile of fluffed up currency would be much better. The whole point of sacraments is that ordinary things, everyday things, are being transformed by God into the means of God's self-communication. Sacraments are about incarnation, about God being present in and among and through the ordinary, transforming the mundane, fulfilling it, not destroying it.

The offertory is one of the places where the emotional connection to the liturgy breaks down for many people. These gifts of bread and wine, money and effort are supposed to stand in for our whole lives. If the elements that are collected and placed on the altar look churchy and artificial, we are in danger of an insufficient identification with the gifts of offering. What you do with your time, how you earn your living, what you obsess about, what you dream about, and what you dread, all that is daily bread. The things that you enjoy, that give life savor and zest, all that is wine. All these things we place upon the altar.

This connection between daily life and the offering of the people at the Eucharist was more vivid in the early days of the church when people would take the bread and wine from their own tables to the church. The deacons would collect the offerings of the people, place enough on the holy table for the communion, and save the rest for distribution for the poor. I am not quite sure how to regain this deep sense of connection between this holy table and the kitchen table, but it is a connection that needs to be revived. It does help when people in the congregation make the bread. There are even congregations where the people make the wine. The problem is that most of us are so removed from bread baking and winemaking that these things that were so ordinary in the ancient world are exotic to us and therefore somewhat unreal. But bread and wine here are precisely a stand in for our most humble daily realities. Christ wants our tables, the kitchen table, the dining room table, the conference room table, the table in the cafeteria and the factory lunch room, to be his table, and when the bread and wine are brought forward by representatives of the people at the offering, we are bringing our lives to him so that he can fill them with his Life.

Alexander Schmemann, in his exquisite commentary on the Eucharist, points out that Adam and Eve in the Garden of Eden were made for a ministry of offering and blessing. Each animal, each plant, every creature, was held up to God and celebrated as a gift of God's love and a communication of God's life to humankind. The existence of humanity in the Garden was a priestly existence, an existence of grateful offering to God. We fell from that vocation. We forgot who we were and what we were made for. We began to crave the world as a thing in itself. The Creation became an idol instead of a means of feasting on God's love. We started to accumulate things as ends in themselves instead of as a means of growing in our knowledge and love of God. Jesus has come to restore us to our original vocation. In him and through him we now bring the world again to God, and the Creation, beginning with bread and wine, again becomes the bread of heaven and the cup of salvation. Ordinary people become again kings and queens of Creation (to care for God's handiwork), priests giving thanks in the cosmic Eucharist, blessing God and feasting on his Love. It is so terribly important that the offering be real, meaningful, and costly, and that we understand that we are presenting these things so that the dignity of human nature and the sanctity of the human vocation of praise and adoration can be restored through the action of Christ. We are presenting these gifts so that through Christ the world will once again become the sacred means by which God nourishes and intoxicates us with his Love.

For all that we offer our own lives it is well to remember that in the end it is only Christ that we offer. That we can come at all and place our gifts upon the altar and offer our selves, our souls and bodies depends upon God spilling the life-giving blood of his Love in the life, death, and resurrection of Jesus. In the offering, we are returning thanks for what has already been given once and for all in Jesus Christ. This will become quite clear and explicit in the prayer of consecration.

The Holy Table. The deacon receives the elements and sets the altar. One paten (plate) of bread and one chalice of wine are placed on a cloth called a corporal in the center of the altar. If more bread and wine are needed, they are placed in other containers in a position that does not distract from the symbolism that we though many are one body and eat of one loaf and drink of one cup (1 Cor. 10:16–17). You may notice that the minister setting the altar pours a little water into the chalice of wine. This is a very ancient custom. In part it simply represents the custom of wine drinking in the time of Jesus. Wine mixed with water was the drink for ordinary meals. In the mind of the church it has taken on a special meaning—St. Cyprian speaks of the water as a symbol for the people. Sofia Cavalletti tells the story of a little boy who was given a small chalice to fill with wine and water as part of his church school. He performed this exercise over and over; when the teacher tried to interest him in other material, he rebelled. Finally, after many repetitions, he turned to the teacher and said, "It takes a lot of wine and a little water because we must lose ourselves in Jesus." This is a pretty good paraphrase of St. Cyprian.

Lavabo. Often just before the priest starts the prayer of Great Thanksgiving, he or she will pause for hand washing. This looks a bit more esoteric than it is. A server holds a bowl called a *lavabo* bowl and pours water over the priest's fingers. The priest dries his or her hands on a small linen towel and proceeds with the service. This ceremonial is not practiced in every church. It is functional for the priest to wash his or her hands before handling food. The ceremony also is a sign that the priest is not worthy to stand in the place of Christ and pray the prayer of Christ, and that it is only because of God's washing love and forgiveness that the priest can stand in this place and do these fearsome things. The ceremony is called the *lavabo* after the opening word in the Latin version of Psalm 26 that was recited in the Roman Mass at this point, "I wash my hands in the waters of innocence that I may go around the altar of my God."

Now the altar, the Holy Table, has been prepared. We are ready to pray.

8

The Great Thanksgiving

THE PRAYER that follows the preparation of the altar is called the Great Thanksgiving. It is the prayer of blessing through which bread and wine become for us the body and blood of Christ. At this point the whole congregation should be standing. This demonstrates that the prayer is the prayer of all the people, of the gathered body.

The Sursum Corda. The opening of the Great Thanksgiving is a dialogue, an ancient hymn called in Latin the *sursum corda,* which means "lift up your hearts." It is a very ancient hymn and was used in synagogue worship. The heart in the language of the Bible is not just an organ for pumping blood; it is the center of the human person. The heart is the essence of human identity. "Lift up your hearts. We lift them up to the Lord." Because Jesus has identified with us we can identify with him. We willingly and freely and eagerly identify ourselves with Jesus the Christ, crucified for our sake, raised from the dead, sitting at the right hand of God. In Jesus our human nature, our human identity, has become re-identified with God. To cast our lot with Jesus is to be reunited in him with the Father. In the Eucharist we are ascending with Jesus to the Father. The Eucharist is the worship of heaven and of the Kingdom of God. When we join ourselves with Christ in his perfect offering to the Father we are no longer in this world. In this world the human heart is not lifted up to God. In this world God is forgotten and the way to God is forgotten. Even when the desire to lift our hearts up to God is awakened, human beings cannot manage to do this. It is beyond them. Their efforts go awry and fail and turn into idolatry, and idolatry always requires human sacrifice. But God has sacrificed himself for us so that we can lift our hearts up to him. He has come down to us so that we may ascend with him. When we make this identification and begin this prayer we are no longer in this world. We are out of this world. We are in heaven. We are in the Kingdom.

This sounds, I am sure, so mystical as to be bizarre. It all hangs on what defines location for you. If the idea of location is exhausted by street address then it is hard to understand how the congregation is lifted up to heaven without a change in address. But there are all kinds of ways of locating oneself and address is only one of them. Where are you today? Are you down? Are you up? Are you lost? Are you found? These are perfectly comprehensible questions, are they not? If we are in love and charity with each other and if we are lifting our hearts, identifying our very selves with Christ and are with him and in him, then we are where he is and where he is, there is heaven, there is the Kingdom of God. Certainly, the old world, the old order, the world that is not Kingdom, is never totally left behind, but nevertheless in the Eucharist time opens upon eternity and we experience a taste of heaven on earth. That we are joining in the worship of heaven will be more clear when we share the song of the angels, called in Latin the *sanctus*,

Holy, Holy, Holy. In, with, and through Christ we shall be partakers in this Eucharist of the worship of heaven.

The Proper Preface. At this point on Sundays and at other times as appointed, a special prayer or preface is inserted. This is one of the points where persons new to Eucharistic worship often become confused. They have finally mastered the art of juggling hymnbook, prayer book, and bulletin. They have found the appropriate page again after the sermon and perhaps an offertory anthem, and are cruising along at flank speed following every word. They turn from page 361 to the next page but can find none of the words the priest is saying. Where did the celebrant go? The celebrant went to page 377, to a list of proper prefaces. The entire prayer from the offertory to the conclusion of the consecration is called the Great Thanksgiving. The priest has called the people to join together (page 361) in this prayer by lifting up their hearts to God the Father, through the Son, in the power of the Spirit. "Let us give thanks to the Lord our God," the priest says, and the people respond, "It is right to give him thanks and praise." Now, in the preface for the day, the priest reminds the congregation of one of the many reasons why it is right to give God thanks and praise. The first proper preface listed on page 377, Of God the Father, reminds us to give thanks because the Father is the source of light and life who made us in his image and has called us to new life in Jesus Christ our Lord. There are proper prefaces for the Son and for the Spirit. Any of these can be used on Sundays when the rubrics do not direct another of the proper prefaces. There are prefaces for each of the seasons of the church year. The preface for Advent celebrates the coming of Christ at Christmas and at the end of time to judge the living and the dead. The preface for the Incarnation is used at Christmastime. There is a preface for Epiphany, for Lent, Holy Week, Good Friday, Easter, Ascension, and Pentecost. In addition there are prefaces for special occasions such as the feast of a martyr or an Apostle. By this changing use of these prefaces, different themes and blessings of the faith are brought to the attention of the congregation. This is yet another protection from the tendency of preachers, teachers, and whole congregations to become fixated on one aspect of the faith, the cross for instance, to the exclusion of some other aspect, such as the gift of the Spirit. The proper prefaces help to keep the congregation's great prayer of thanksgiving whole, universal, catholic in the original meaning of the term.

Once the Great Thanksgiving has begun, I believe the less one uses the prayer book the better. Better to look at the altar and listen keenly to the words and memorize the few responses. Yet there can be no one style of praying the Eucharist that will work for all, and some are greatly helped rather than distracted by following in the prayer book. Even for those I recommend not turning to the pages for the preface. It is awkward and the service quickly resumes on original course. Be aware that at this point a short paragraph will be inserted that will sound a theme for special thanksgiving and reverence. Know that it is coming, listen attentively for the few sentences, and pick up in the book again as the service continues on page 362.

Note that prayers C and D (pages 369–376) in the Book of Common Prayer do not use proper prefaces but continue uninterrupted to the Sanctus. A proper preface has not always been a feature of all Eucharistic prayers and neither is it so in this prayer book. They are not an absolutely essential element of the Eucharistic prayer but they are an entirely wholesome one.

Sanctus. Having brought to mind the particular aspect of God's grace and bounty and care highlighted in the preface, the priest continues, "Therefore we praise you, joining our voices with Angels and Archangels and with all the company of heaven, who forever sing this hymn to proclaim the glory of your Name." When we rightly give thanks to God, praise God, and worship God, we are no longer alone. We are united as a congregation to be sure, but we are also part of a greater gathering. We are united with the angels and the company of heaven. Now we are restored. Now we are as whole as it is possible to be this side of the grave. The terrible separation that exists between humanity and God has been overcome. We take our place in union with God's angels and the saints of every generation reveling, luxuriating, in the goodness and loving kindness of God, God's love of us overflowing into awe, wonder, and thanksgiving toward him.

The words of the angels' song are taken from the Book of Revelation (4:8), John of Patmos' vision of the worship of heaven, and from the vision of the prophet Isaiah (6:3) in the temple. This part of the service is called in Latin the *Sanctus*, which is the Latin word for holy. "Holy, Holy, Holy," the angels sing. This is the song that the prophet Isaiah heard when, in a time in which there were no visions and God seemed far away, the prophet went into the temple to pray and had a vision of the Almighty. This is the song that the Apostle John heard in his exile on Patmos as he was granted a vision of heaven. The words tell us that we are approaching the center of the mystery of the Eucharist. We are entering into the presence of God. God himself is coming into our presence. "Heaven and earth are full of your glory," the angels sing and we sing with them. The words remind us of the worship of heaven, of moments of past theophany—the appearing of the elusive and awesome God. They remind us also of the ultimate theophany, the appearing of God, of which we know—the coming of God to be with us and for us in Jesus Christ. In this song of the angels, there is also the echo of the night on which Christ was born and the song of the angels in Luke 2:14. God wants us to know him and has come to us completely self-revealing in a human life, the life of Jesus Christ. Now we are going to meet the Christ that we know already through our Baptism, and through our Christian fellowship, in the peculiarly intimate manner that He has ordained in the breaking of the bread. Bethlehem means "house of bread." As the angels sang on Christmas Eve, so they now sing, and we join with them as this new Bethlehem comes to pass and Christ labors to be born again in his church and in the heart of each member.

Benedictus Qui Venit. The last phrase of the Sanctus is called the *Benedictus* or the *Benedictus Qui Venit,* which is Latin for "Blessed is he that comes." The biblical reference here is Matthew 11:9. Jesus has completed his course of healing and teaching in the countryside and has set his face toward Jerusalem, though he knows that it will mean his death. He enters Jerusalem on the back of a donkey, which fulfills the prophecy of Zechariah that the Messiah when he comes will be humble and righteous, not like the arrogant and corrupt kings who lord it over their subjects with displays of chariots and horses. The crowd goes wild when they see Jesus riding into the city. The Messiah, the savior, the promised one of God has come and will certainly now set things to rights, even old scores, overthrow the Romans, punish the enemies of Israel, and redistribute the wealth. Jesus is not this kind of savior and the next day in their disappointment and rage this same crowd that shouted, "Hosanna" will shout, "crucify him." These lines carry a poignant meaning. They speak, as does all of the Sanctus, of the joyful expectation of the approach of God in Christ. They also are full of the shadow of the cross and foreshadow the theme that will be treated more thoroughly in the body of the prayer of consecration that when the long hoped for savior comes, when God reveals himself to humankind in the life of Jesus, the Christ is crucified. We who sing praises now are reminded of how quickly our adoration can turn to contempt and betrayal.

Many people cross themselves at the words, "Blessed is he that comes in the name of the Lord." It is an old custom, though not from the earliest years of the church. The sign of the cross is always a sign of the identification of the life of the individual believer with the life of Christ. Here it seems a not unfitting recognition that we sing our praises in the shadow of the cross, and a prayer that we will be faithful followers in the way of the cross and not betrayers of Christ. Unlike the crowds of old, we at least know that salvation lies in following the humble, suffering savior and not in a triumphal avenger. God knows that we find it hard to follow this man who rides on the donkey, washes the feet of his disciples, and gives up his life as a ransom for many. God knows and forgives. I have said before that signs and ceremonials should not be a stumbling block for anyone and should be determined on the basis of what aids rather than impedes piety, reverence, and worship. This cannot be the same for everyone. Yet there are times when a few lines of the Eucharistic prayer are so overfull of meaning that some response, some gesture is called forth from the depths of the human heart. From the outside, signs of the cross, bowing, and the like can look like vanity and superstition. From another point of view they are a humble attempt to respond to the depth of feeling which true worship stirs up in the heart of the believer. The sign of the cross here is not liked by some liturgical scholars because it cannot be attributed to antiquity. It can be attributed to an instinct to acknowledge the profundity of the prayer.

9

The Unforgetting

A *NAMNESIS.* FOR convenience, different parts of the prayer are known by different names. Inevitably these designations are somewhat arbitrary and vary in their use with different commentators. The body of the prayer is sometimes called the prayer of consecration, the canon, or the preface (as distinguished from the proper preface). I have chosen to use the designation anamnesis, which means in Greek, "the un-forgetting." A person who has lost his memory has amnesia and literally does not know who he or she is. Anamnesis is the opposite of this condition. Anamnesis is the un-forgetting that causes a person or a people to remember and thereby regain identity. Perhaps when you were a teenager and were just beginning to go out on your own, your mother or father stood in the door as you were leaving and said, "Remember who you are." Likewise the prophets of Israel when they wanted to recall God's people to the Torah, the way of life, would call Israel to remembrance. "Remember how God brought you up out of the house of slavery with signs and wonders and with an outstretched arm. Remember, O Israel, who you are and the sacred vocation for which you have been created." In this part of the prayer (page 362), the whole of salvation history is rehearsed. The mighty deeds of God on behalf of God's people are brought to mind in praise, awe and thanksgiving, deeds culminating in the sending of the savior and the remembrance of Christ's death and resurrection and especially in remembrance of those things that Christ did and said on the night in which he was betrayed.

One more thing needs to be said about this word anamnesis. It means to remember or literally to un-forget. When we come to the words of institution, Jesus says, "Do this in remembrance of me." The Greek word translated as remembrance is anamnesis. Unfortunately the English word remembrance does not have the same nuance as the Greek word it translates. An English paraphrase might be, "do this for recalling me," or, "do this for making me present." This prayer of un-forgetting on which we are embarking finds its completion as we have our identity restored as brothers and sisters of the living and risen Lord, present in our midst in this peculiar and unique way as He promised.

Just after the completion of the Sanctus, there is an instruction in italics, a rubric (page 362), which reads, "The people stand or kneel." This is an awkward moment for many people new to Eucharistic worship. In most congregations there is a custom that is followed by most of the worshipers. The confusing thing for the newcomer is that it is rare to find total uniformity in any congregation. If most people kneel at this point and those nearest you stand, what do you do? My suggestion is that you follow the usage of the majority of the congregation until you develop your own preference. It is quite clear that standing is the more ancient posture. In the time of St. John Chrysostom (349–407 AD), there was a prohibition against kneeling in the church during the great fifty days of Eastertide. During the Middle Ages, kneeling became common as a sign of reverence for the sacred act of consecration. People were bowing down in the presence of God. The liturgical movement that gave rise to the new prayer book sought to restore as much as possible the forms and practices of antiquity, so that our worship would resemble the worship of the earliest Christians. There is somewhat less confidence now among scholars that the practice of the early church was as uniform as was supposed when the 1979 book was being prepared. Some think that standing makes it easier to see the action at the altar; some feel that standing together conveys the feeling of a community gathered in a common action better than kneeling. Some think standing is a better sign that the gathered church is a priestly people offering its supreme act of thanksgiving each according to his or her order.

In one congregation where I was rector, I carefully led the parish in a change of its custom of kneeling during the prayer of consecration to standing. I explained the history and theology, and we introduced the change gradually, at first standing only during the Great Fifty Days after Easter. At the end of a year the change was complete. In retrospect I wonder about the value of the change. The most notable consequence was that older people complained of fatigue from so much standing and the smallest children seemed more unhappy and fidgety. It seemed to me there was little or nothing added in terms of praise, thanksgiving, and joy, and that there was a perceptible drop in the level of reverence. I thought one or two of the most skeptical members of the congregation had developed a gloating smirk that was not there before. C.S. Lewis once said that the average lay person is more interested in whether something in the liturgy is meat or poison than in its original location on the menu. To that might be added that one person's meat is another's poison. Great latitude should be left in such things to accommodate the piety of different individuals and congregations.

"Holy and gracious Father": Notice that the prayer is addressed to the Father. All Christian prayer is to the Father through the Son and in the power of the Spirit. This is of course true for the quintessential prayer, the Holy Eucharist. We hear again the history of salvation. God in his infinite love made us for himself and endowed us with a measure of the freedom, creativity, and love that is part of the divine life. We misused our freedom and turned from God. The biblical language for this tragic turn in human nature is the Fall. The Bible says we fell into sin and became cut off from God. Because we are cut off from God we are subject to, that is, under the control of, evil and death, death of the spirit and even death of the body. The scriptures teach that none of these are the natural, the God-intended, destiny of human nature. They are unnatural, against God's intention, a self-contrived tragedy. God does not leave us in this terrible predicament, but sends his Son to redeem us. "You, in your mercy, sent Jesus Christ, your only and eternal Son, to share our human nature, to live and die as one of us, to reconcile us to you, the God and Father of all."

Here is the problem and drama of salvation. How is God, who made us to be free, to rescue us from sin and evil without compromising our freedom? It cannot be by a show of power or force. The God of the Bible wants a people who will freely return his love—not by outward compulsion but by an inward compulsion of thanksgiving, of gratitude welling up for the gift God has given us in sending his Son to free us from the power of evil and death. So God, wanting to reconcile us to his purposes and love, sent his eternal Son to share our human nature. The eternal Word of God's love that always and eternally goes out from God to accomplish God's purposes becomes flesh in Jesus. The Word that reveals itself in the history of Israel, in the Ten Commandments, in the words of the prophets, becomes present in the life of Jesus. In Jesus we meet God, the awesome and transcendent ruler of the universe who confronts us with an inescapable call to holiness, righteousness and justice, in one who was tempted in every way as we are and who has lived in our skin, walked in our shoes, and has the deepest sympathy and empathy for us.

In a time when it is taken as axiomatic by many people that all religions speak in different ways of the same "truth," it is important to recognize what a unique and distinctive message is proclaimed in the Christian assertion that God became human in Jesus Christ, and why this proclamation is received as great good news. In a congregation I served, there is a doctor who is a world traveler and who takes very fine photographs of her travels. One time she traveled to Bali, a beautiful country with an ancient spiritual tradition. She shared her photographs with us at the church. One cannot but admire the high sense of morality, truth, and beauty that comes through the cultural artifacts that the doctor shared with us. There was one picture that was very revealing —a picture of a Balinese temple. The temple was a pyramid. Its sides consisted of steep steps. The doctor explained that the steps were designed to be higher than a person could easily reach in order to make a point. The point was that it is very hard, nearly impossible, to climb up to God. The laborious, exhausting, nearly impossible climb to the top of the temple was a metaphor for the human search for God. In the non-biblical religions there is great beauty and truth, but there is a great contrast between the Christian revelation and the non-biblical religions. While men and women are trying with great difficulty to climb up to God, God has come down to be one of us. The knowledge of God, the love of God, the mercy and forgiveness and grace of God are not only for the few, the favored, who can make the climb. God does not want to remain hidden, inaccessible. God wants human beings to know God's love intimately and yet in such a way that they can return to God's ways with free and grateful hearts. This is Gospel. This is great good news.

There is, sadly, more to the story. God reaches across the gulf that separates us from him but we do not embrace God's outstretched hand. When the Savior appears, we reject him. God has not only to become one of us but has also to overcome our hostility to God. Picture this: a child feels rejected by his or her parent. The parent stoops to pick up and comfort the child. The child struggles, even beats against the parent's chest before allowing itself to be comforted. So Christ stretches out his arms on the hard wood of the cross so that the whole world might come within the reach of his saving embrace. God overcomes the hostility of the world not by a show of force or overwhelming power but by the power of the cross, the power of weakness and suffering love. The prayer of consecration speaks of this act of suffering love as "a perfect sacrifice for the whole world."

This persistent, patient love that overcomes and extinguishes hostility and evil is the eternal response of the Son to the Father's goodness and love. This sacrifice is the Father's love returned to him by the Son in the power of the Spirit. In the Eucharist, we are recognizing the gift of this sacrifice poured out for us, and we are joining ourselves with the Son by the power of the Holy Spirit in this sacrifice of praise and thanksgiving to the Father.

When I celebrate the Eucharist, at the words "a perfect sacrifice for the whole world," I point to the elements of bread and wine on the table. What Christ did with his whole ministry and life, that is, offered them to the Father in thanksgiving for the sake of the whole world, Christ did with bread and wine for his disciples on the night in which he was betrayed. On the night in which he was betrayed, he identified the offering of his life, his passion and death which was fast upon him, with this simple offering of bread and wine in such a way that whenever it is offered in his name and with his words, he is one with us and we are one with him in his one act of self-offering which overcomes evil and sin, and reconciles humanity to God as brothers and sisters of the same loving and forgiving Father.

Now the priest places his or her hand upon the bread and then the wine or holds each up, and recites in turn, first for the bread and then for the wine, "the words of institution." These are the words that Christ said on the night in which he was betrayed. By these words of Jesus, this sacrament of his body and blood has been instituted. By these words Jesus has brought into being a means for his disciples then and now to be in communion with his holy and life-giving presence. "This is my Body, which is given for you. Do this for the remembrance of me." "This is my Blood of the new Covenant, which is shed for you and for many for the forgiveness of sins. Whenever you drink it, do this for the remembrance of me." A hard word to explicate, this word "covenant." It means so many things. A covenant is a solemn contract, a set of sacred promises, a set of well-defined relationships and mutual obligations. In our world, where a person's word is cheap and people are cynical about enduring promises and obligations, it is hard to catch the force of this word covenant. Though marriage is under great attack in our time, it is perhaps still the best equivalent. It is as though Christ says, "In my blood, in my life of love poured out for the forgiveness of sins, there is a new marriage between God and humanity. Feed upon my life, drink in this new relationship with God and with each other."

At this point in the service in some parishes, the bread will be elevated and silence kept or perhaps a bell rung after the words of institution over the bread, and again over the wine. This is a medieval custom. It is good in that it betokens great respect for the holiness and sanctity of what is taking place and is a way of underlining the words of Jesus. It is a way of signaling that we are entering into the heart of the holy mystery. At one point in the history of theology there was a great interest in trying to fix the moment of consecration and identify the moment when the bread and wine ceased to be merely mundane and became the body and blood of Christ. In the West this moment became associated with the words of institution. It was the words of the Word that brought about the transformation of the elements. Acts of reverence at this point reflect that theology. In the East the moment of consecration was associated with the prayer asking the Holy Spirit to sanctify the elements and make them the Body and Blood of Christ. Demonstrating our reverence towards Christ's gift of himself to us in the Eucharist through the bread and wine is a good thing. Parishes will vary in their custom of these things and rightly so. It is good also to remember from time to time the ideas and sentiments that originally gave rise to particular ceremonial, and to ask if our acts of reverence still express our best understanding. Anglicans have traditionally been disinterested in localizing a moment of consecration and have looked to the whole prayer including the Great Amen, which is the response of the people, as the necessary condition for consecration. It is in my opinion more characteristically Anglican to elevate and reverence the elements after the prayer of consecration is complete and the people have said, Amen, let it be so.

Immediately after the words of institution the celebrant says, "Therefore we proclaim the mystery of faith:" (page 363). In light of all that God has done for us in the whole history of salvation and especially in the life and death of Jesus Christ, having remembered who we are and who God is, we proclaim the mystery of faith. The word mystery here means the holy, surprising, and inexpressibly gracious act of God on our behalf. Mystery is the word that is often used to translate the Greek word *mysterion*, which can mean miracle or sacrament. Our faith is that in these mysteries God acts for our healing and salvation. Notice that this summary of the Christian faith is not a list of the teachings of Jesus. It is not a list of doctrines or concepts. Our faith is that God has done things, has acted. God has entered totally into human life and identified totally with us in our lostness and rebellion and in our captivity to evil. God has come as savior, as Christ. Christ has died for us, at our hands, taking to himself the full bitterness of our evil. Christ has risen. The life and love of Christ has overcome the death-dealing hate in us. God has raised Jesus from the grave. Christ will come again. This Kingdom of which we have a foretaste in this Eucharist will come in fullness and power. The relationship of peace, love, and justice with each other and God in Christ that we celebrate in this sacrament is God's will for the whole creation. He will bring his will to perfection and completion. There will come a time when the Son will completely restore the Creation and offer this completed work to the Father in the power of the Spirit. The light of that future radiates in this Eucharist. We proclaim this faith together. We are identifying ourselves as people who live in the light of this awesome reality. We know that the savior has come and has died and is risen and is making all things new. We are part of this new creation and we look forward to the perfection of God's work of love in the life of the world to come. Sacrificial love which brings life out of death and makes all things new, which tokens and promises a new future—that is the paradigm, the pattern of God's dealing with us, that is the mystery of our faith.

The celebrant continues, "We celebrate the memorial of our redemption, O Father, in this sacrifice of praise and thanksgiving. Recalling his death, resurrection, and ascension, we offer you these gifts." I understand that when a person has had a serious head injury, the patient sometimes has to learn to move and walk all over again. The therapist will move the arms and legs of the patient over and over again in a particular way, which instills in the patient's nervous system the building blocks of autonomous movement. This process is called re-patterning. The patient's brain is literally being reprogrammed so that the patient can ultimately regain the use of a function that has become impaired. We are impaired. Our human function is damaged. Our humanity lurches and wobbles and is unsteady on its feet. Sometimes when we know we should act in a certain way, and act decisively, we find we are paralyzed. In Jesus God is re-patterning the human race, putting into us those building blocks of goodness and holiness so that ultimately we freely return praise and love to God and share justice and peace with each other. The therapist's work with the patient is a remembering, a memorial. This is the sort of thing we mean when we say that we celebrate the memorial of our redemption. It is not memorial in the sense of memorial stone, a monument to what once happened. It is memorial in the sense of active remembering, of reliving, re-experiencing. It is memorial in the sense of a real and healing intervention that restores and empowers.

Now recalling, remembering in this active, vital sense, and not merely as a human act alone but by the power of God's Holy Spirit working in us, the self-giving death of Christ, his victory over evil, sin and death, his new and risen life and his ascension, his raising of our life to the life of the Father—all these are at work in us to restore and redeem us. Only by virtue of this remembering, this repatterning, this work of God in us, are we able to offer God thanks and praise. All we have to offer in thanks and praise are these gifts. These gifts are our lives in the process of being redeemed and restored by Christ's life. Here the priest points to or lifts up the bread and the wine. Christ's offering of himself to the Father on our behalf, his offering of bread and wine on the night in which he was betrayed, our offering of the bread and wine in his name, according to his words, our joining with him in his holy offering, all these things have become one in this prayer, in this Eucharist. We are praying in Christ and he is praying in us.

The Epiclesis. Now comes the prayer to the Holy Spirit, the Epiclesis, which was mentioned earlier. The priest makes the sign of the cross over the elements, or perhaps holds the hands crossed over the elements, and prays that the Father will sanctify the bread and wine by the power of the Holy Spirit to "be for your people the Body and Blood of your Son, the holy food and drink of new and unending life in him." It is the role of the Holy Spirit to bring to perfection the work of the Son. The work of the Son is to restore the Creation so that it once again becomes the feast of God's love and we once again become the priests of that feast, recognizing its holiness and giving thanks to our Provider. This restoration of all things begins with this bread and wine and through the power of the Spirit all that we have prayed over them is brought to completion and perfection.

The Epiclesis, the invocation of the Holy Spirit, continues. "Sanctify us also." Here is the most appropriate place in all of Christian liturgy to make the sign of the cross. Here we ask that by the power of the Spirit we will be transformed and become ourselves the Body of Christ, the life-giving Blood of his love in the world. Here we pray that the Spirit will complete his work in us and bring us to the perfection of the Kingdom.

This is our prayer. We ask it through Christ, by his intercession. We ask it with him. We join with him in his sacrifice of praise and thanksgiving. We ask it in him because we are his body by the unifying power of the Holy Spirit and are brought with him to give you, Father, all honor and glory. This feast of love, praise, thanksgiving, this celebration of holy communion with each other and the Father through the Son and in the power of the Spirit, this abundant participation in the eternal conversation and exchange of divine love, is what we do now and shall do forever. Here the elements may be elevated as the offering of Christ to the Father and our offering of this Eucharist in and with him become one.

At this point the people say Amen. This is called the Great AMEN. In the Book of Common Prayer it is the only Amen that is all in capital letters. The culmination of the most solemn and sacred prayer in Christian liturgy is the people saying Amen, let it be so. In the Anglican tradition, the priest cannot celebrate the Eucharist alone. There must be a congregation. There must be a faithful people who say let it be so. Let this work of God come to pass in and through us. Amen. At this point the most reverential and celebratory ceremonial is appropriate. I place the elements that have been elevated on the altar and make a profound bow. Singing the Great Amen is a good way of underlining the crescendo of praise that these words denote. The ringing of bells and the use of incense would not be amiss. Most important is that the response of the people, their Amen! be hearty, full voiced, and full of awe and reverence at that which is taking place.

10

The Our Father

IMMEDIATELY AFTER the Great Amen comes the invitation to pray the prayer our Savior taught. There are two versions of the invitation to pray. One uses the language of the older Books of Common Prayer, and says "And now, as our Savior Christ has taught us, we are bold to say"—this invitation goes with a version of the Lord's Prayer that is in more traditional language. I like both the traditional invitation and the traditional version of the prayer. The contemporary invitation is straightforward and easy to understand: "As our Savior Christ has taught us, we now pray," but the older invitation makes the connection between the work of the Savior and his teaching. By his death and resurrection, which has just been represented to us in the Eucharistic prayer, Jesus has reconciled us to his Father, brought us to the place where we can share with him the Life he has with the Father in the power of the Spirit. So with him and through him and in him—now reconciled to God and to each other, we can do what would otherwise be gross impertinence. We can indeed with boldness say "Our Father."

One of the things that were striking about Jesus to his disciples was his life of prayer. He is depicted as having a deep

and intense life of prayer. He prays before his baptism, before choosing the disciples, after ministering to the crowds.
He takes time apart, often in lonely places, for prayer. Jesus
has closeness, has union, with the Father, and this closeness is palpable to those around him. They want to be able
to pray like this. It is also customary that a rabbi teaches
particular prayers to his disciples. These prayers mark off
these disciples as a distinctive religious community, as followers of this rabbi. John taught his disciples how to pray;
teach us. It is likely that both of these motivations are at
work in the question put to Jesus by the disciples. He said to
them, "When you pray, say Father, hallowed be your name."
First we need to understand that this instruction in prayer
is being given not to individuals only but to a community,
the community of the disciples, the nascent Church. This
is of course the way that we are to pray as individuals but it
is also the way we are to pray as a new people, a new community, a new family, the family which has been brought
into being by the death and resurrection of the Lord. There
is no teaching in the New Testament that is not lit from behind by the passion and death of the Lord and by the empty
tomb and the resurrection appearances. Everything that he
taught them takes on a new character—a new luminescence
in the light of the death and resurrection—including the
teaching on prayer. The original disciples shared these characteristics: they were called, chosen of God, not because of
any merit or greatness of their own; they were granted the
privilege of being with Jesus, hearing his teaching, witnessing his power, and they all betrayed and deserted him. They
ran away, they like Peter denied him publicly. To these the
crucified and risen One appeared, greeting them with for-

giveness and love and breathing into them his Spirit, the Spirit he shares with the Father to whom he prays. Because of the costly gift of this Spirit, we are able to say "Father." "Our Father," we say, in deep solidarity with each other in the gratuitous mercy of God who has called us together. We have solidarity in sin, in our resistance and rebellion and betrayal of God's claim upon our lives, our batting away of the embrace of the Savior—solidarity in being recipients of costly forgiveness and an undeserved second chance. We have solidarity in the gift of the Spirit, which allows us to say with him and with our brothers and sisters, "Our Father."

"Hallowed be Thy name." In the scriptures a man's name is his reputation. It is how the person is regarded, how they are remembered. Abraham does not have a son and he is worried that his name will die out and be forgotten. The phrase "Hallowed be your name" is a petition that God will act in such a way that people will have awe and reverence toward God, that they will regard properly who God is and what the Father has done. One of the characteristics of the Christian faith is that it has through and through the characteristic of already and not yet. Already those of us who have identified ourselves with Christ have died with Christ to sin; already we are a new creation, and yet we struggle to put to death the old way of life with all its lying, cheating, stealing, and killing,—to live the new life he has come at such great price to offer us. Already we have what St. Paul calls an *arabon*, a down payment of the Kingdom that is coming. God has already hallowed God's name. The Father has acted in an astonishing way to demonstrate his power and might. He has acted to bring men and women to a humble acknowledgement of his majesty and power.

The Father has done this in, with, and through the sending of the Son to meet human wickedness with sacrifice and love, to bring new life through death. This prayer has been answered by the death and resurrection of the Savior who gives his life as a ransom for many and rises with healing in his wings, as the prophet Malachi says (4:2).

The prayer remains to be prayed and to be answered in that we who are witnesses to the love and power of God made known in Christ might so live toward God, toward each other, and toward an unbelieving world, that God's name would be honored and hallowed among people on our account.

"Give us today our daily bread." There is a dispute among the scholars about the exact meaning of daily; there appears to be an Aramaic idiom behind the Greek. It could mean "day by day"; it could mean tomorrow's bread today, referring to the bread of the Kingdom, the Kingdom Jesus has been teaching about, which is at hand, already but not yet. The phrase causes me to think of a particular loaf of bread. When I was in high school, I had the great privilege of living in a Jewish home for a year. Each Friday there was a Sabbath meal. The best china and silver were brought out. If there was quarreling in the house, the feud had to be mended before supper; forgiveness must be offered and accepted. The Sabbath meal was a Kingdom meal—an already but not yet anticipation of the Kingdom that God will bring in at last when His kingdom has come on earth as it is in heaven, when, as the prophet Isaiah says, the lion will lie down with the lamb and they will not hurt or destroy on all my holy mountain, when every tear shall be wiped away from every eye, and death and mourning will be no more—where men and women of all races are reconciled to God and to each other. There will be a feast of fat things and the best wine. At the Sabbath meal there is a special bread. You see it in stores; it is called Challah bread, a rich eggy bread. At the Sabbath meals I attended, everyone would be given a piece of bread and a cup of wine before the blessing was said. Then just before the blessing, the special knife used to cut the Sabbath bread would be folded into its handle, because, it was explained to me, at the feast of the Kingdom there must be no weapon in sight. When we pray the Lord's Prayer, we are praying for daily sustenance—it is a very real plea for vast swaths of the human race—but we also pray for this bread of the Kingdom, this bread of reconciliation that brings us to peace with God and with each other.

So it is meet and right that we should then pray for forgiveness, for the reconciliation with God that makes it possible to forgive each other. If I have been pardoned by God for living as his enemy, shall I not extend this pardon to my own enemies? Thank God he has not treated me *quid pro quo*, tit for tat. The way to thank God is to offer forgiveness and mercy, in such a way that God's name is hallowed. You may remember how moved the world was by the way the Amish treated the family of the man who had murdered their children.

"And do not bring us to the time of trial." Each day we are tempted to live contrary to this prayer. There will be a day when God will finally overthrow all those who resist his purposes. There will come a day when everything will be tested and tried, and there will be a final sorting, of wheat from tares, of sheep from goats. Save us from that trial, Lord—preserve us and keep us forever.

11

The Breaking of the Bread

After the recitation of the Our Father, the next heading in bold type is "The Breaking of the Bread" (page 364). The name for this part of the service is the fraction. Many well-known pieces of music have been written to accompany this part of the service; they are called fraction anthems. One of them appears immediately below the heading, following the instruction to the celebrant to break the consecrated bread and that a period of silence be kept after the breaking. The fraction anthem can be sung or said: "Alleluia. Christ our Passover is sacrificed for us." The response is: "Therefore let us keep the feast. Alleluia."

When God rescued the people of Israel from their slavery under Pharaoh, God gave instructions that each family should choose a spotless lamb to be prepared for a family meal. Some of the blood of the lamb was to be painted on the lintel over the entrance to their homes. Thus the blood of the lamb consecrated, that is, set apart the people as God's people. When the angel of death passed through the Egyptians, God's people, consecrated by the blood of the Passover lamb, were saved. In that night, God triumphed over Pharaoh, and Pharaoh relented and let the people go. They were prepared and strengthened for the journey by feeding on the lamb and by the unleavened bread they had been instructed to bake. It was food for the journey, the journey of deliverance, the Exodus meal.

Even as they set out, Pharaoh pursued them with the intent of wiping them off the face of the earth. With Pharaoh on one side and the Red Sea on the other side, God made a way out of no way and parted the waters that the people might escape death and take up a new life as God's people. From the mountain, God led them on with a pillar of flame by night and a pillar of cloud by day, through the desert and through many trials and temptations. He established them in the promised land as his people, to serve his purposes.

Now this whole series of events—the deliverance from Pharaoh, through the night of death and through the Red Sea, the giving of the Law, the providential leading to the promised land, this whole thing is the Exodus—the Passover. Jesus is the new Moses, and he has defeated the forces that stood behind all the pharaohs, all the empires of death that have ever been or shall ever be. Jesus is our Passover lamb; we have been washed in his blood and set apart as his people. Jesus our Passover stands between us and the principalities and powers of sin and evil and death. He has by his sacrifice of love made a way out of no way and given us a new way of life. He has given us his Spirit to live this life, which is a life of restored human dignity. He promises to lead us at last, through many trials and temptations, to the Promised Land in his Kingdom.

After the first Exodus the people of Israel were instructed to keep an annual Passover feast. A lamb would be prepared in the same way as on the night in which they were delivered, and by virtue of a ritual meal in conjunction with the re-presentation, the re-telling, of the story of their redemption, the saving event of the first Exodus was made a present reality that could be experienced today. Christ our Passover has been sacrificed for us. Through the ritual meal which he gave us on the night in which he was betrayed, in conjunction with the re-presentation of what God has done for us in, with, and through his Son, the Passover which Jesus accomplished in his death and resurrection are made present for us in such a way that it becomes a living reality for us today. Thus we respond, "Therefore let us keep the feast," the feast of our salvation. During penitential seasons, the alleluias may be omitted as a way of preparing to encounter afresh the good news of our redemption.

The rubric (instruction) says that before the fraction anthem is offered, the consecrated host is broken and a moment of silence is kept. This needs to be a deep and profound silence—a moment of stillness in which the action of breaking the bread sums up and brings before us all to which we just said "Amen," and the reality that Christ cannot share his life with us—that the life that is in him cannot get into us—without his giving of his body to be broken for us, without his pouring out of his life in love and obedience to the last. Without the sacrifice of love, the feast of reconciliation is not possible.

After the fraction anthem is said, or during the singing of it, is the appropriate time to break the bread further and fill the vessels for the distribution of the consecrated bread and wine. This activity is not a utilitarian afterthought, but is part of the re-presentation of that which the Lord did on the night in which he was betrayed. He took the gifts, blessed them, broke them, and gave them to his disciples. In the story from St. Luke of the Emmaus Road that has been our guide throughout this journey, the disciples listened as Jesus rehearsed the whole plan of salvation throughout history. They listened as he blessed the bread, as he had done on the night in which he was betrayed, and they recognized the Risen Lord when he broke the bread. By that action of breaking he brought them once again to the foot of the cross, which is the one place from which the reality of the resurrection can be perceived and from which the power of the new life can be grasped in faith.

After any additional patens (plates for communion bread) and any additional chalices that may be necessary are filled, the priest lifts the chalice and paten. If other priests or deacons are assisting, they may be given a paten or chalice to lift as well. The celebrant says, "The Gifts of God for the People of God." This is the invitation for the faithful to come forward to receive communion. The celebrant may add the words, "Take them in remembrance that Christ died for you, and feed on him in your hearts by faith, with thanksgiving." This phrase is from the classic Book of Common Prayer. Its purpose is to guide the communicants toward a proper understanding of the real presence of Christ in the Eucharist.

Some think that what divides Protestants from Roman Catholics is that Roman Catholics believe in the real presence of Christ in the Eucharist and Protestants do not. It is rather the case that Roman Catholics, Anglicans, Lutherans, the Reformed such as Presbyterians, and the Eastern Orthodox churches all alike affirm a real presence of Christ in the Eucharist. Those churches that come out of the Anabaptist tradition regard the sacrament as a sign or memorial, and the language of real presence is foreign to them.

At the time of the English Reformation, the argument between the Church of England and the Church of Rome was not about whether Christ was present in a unique way to the faithful in the sacrament, but how. The dominant Roman Catholic theory at the time was the theory of transubstantiation—the bread and the wine still appear as bread and wine but their substance has been changed into the substance of Christ's body and blood. The disputes of the time are complex and there are questions about the relationship between the official theology of the Roman Church and how the doctrine was understood or misunderstood by the mass of the people. The time of the Reformation was a time of hot controversy; each side in the dispute had a tendency to put the worst possible construction on the definitions of the other side. This is not the place for a long essay on the controversies over Eucharistic theology. The concern of the Reformers was that the popular understanding of the means of the presence of Christ in the Eucharist lent itself to a superstitious and magical view of the sacrament, such that there was a danger that congregations would become more focused on the mystery, the change in the elements, than on the purpose of the Eucharist: that we might feed on Christ, be reconciled to God and to each other, and be strengthened for the living of the Christian life.

The Eucharistic theology of the classical Anglican theologians stresses the real presence of Christ in the Eucharist, and affirms that the sacrament conveys, in the prayer book phrase, "all the benefits of his passion," and that the holy communion is a real feeding on the new and risen humanity of the resurrected Lord. The theology behind the prayer is also cautious about defining a theory about how Christ is present, and wants to avoid a crudely materialistic view. In classical Anglican sacramental thinking, a real presence of Christ in the Eucharist is affirmed that is spiritual and sacramental. We are inclined to think of spiritual and real as opposites. The theological tradition that stands behind the prayer book uses the words sacramental, spiritual, and real interchangeably. Christ is present in the Eucharist really and truly in a mode that is proper to a sacrament. The way in which we lay hold of this reality is by faith—by trusting in it, leaning on it, using it. There is a saying attributed to Queen Elizabeth the First that I believe does sum up the classical Anglican approach to the sacrament: "He was the Word that spake it, And what the Word did make it, I do believe in and take it." There is no doubt that Cranmer taught that the proper way to take in the presence of Christ in the Eucharist is by faith and with thanksgiving.

I prefer the shorter invitation. An exaggerated piety (tending toward superstition) about the Eucharistic elements is not the great problem of our time. Rather, our problem is that we lose our grip on the supernatural and transcendent in such a way that the reception of communion becomes mundane, lacking in both the awe and the promise that are inherent in an encounter with the living God. I appreciate the theology behind the longer invitation but I think the explanation it contains could be given at other times. Sometimes it is better not to break into the language of worship with the language of instruction.

As soon as the invitation to communion is given, the ministers reverently receive communion and deliver communion to the people. In most churches in the Anglican tradition, there is a communion rail and the people come forward and kneel down to receive. In other places, communion is given to the people standing, as they come up to the communion station one by one.

The communicant puts his or her palms together to receive the consecrated bread. If the person is right-handed, it works well to place the left hand in the right hand, palms up. Then a right-handed person is able to pick up the consecrated bread from the palm of the left hand and reverently consume it. The process can be reversed for a left-handed person. When the wine is offered, the communicant should place a hand on the base of the chalice and guide the chalice to their lips to take a sip of the consecrated wine. In some churches, many of the communicants will dip the bread into the chalice instead of drinking from the chalice. This is known as intinction. Sometimes a minister will offer a separate, usually smaller, cup for those wishing to intinct. People have different reasons for practicing intinction. For some it is the desire to minimize the consumption of alcohol. Communicants who are not able to consume wine at all can either leave the rail or the communion line immediately after receiving the bread or cross their arms and bow their heads when the chalice is offered and the minister will go to the next person in line. Other people and parishes practice intinction out of concern for the possible spread of disease from the common cup. During the early days of the Aids epidemic, when less was known about how that disease is transmitted, many congregations that had not previously practiced intinction took it up. It is my practice to accommodate those who wish to intinct. The communicant holds the consecrated bread in front of them and it is obvious to the minister of the cup that they wish to intinct. But I also explain from time to time that it is a very powerful symbol of our unity in and with Christ that the bread we share is one loaf and the cup we drink is one cup.

The combination of wine and silver or gold in a chalice creates an environment that is inhospitable to germs. In the tradition of churchmanship in which I have been formed, the priest reverently consumes any of the consecrated wine left in the chalice at the end of Communion. If it were likely that one would get a dread disease from sharing the common cup, it should have long ago happened to me. Obviously the whole matter is one that needs great pastoral sensitivity.

Nevertheless I recommend communion from the common cup. Not too many years ago, two videos were shown again and again on television. One video was of a black man—Rodney King—being beaten by white policemen. The other video was of a white truck driver, Reginald Denny, being beaten by black men. I pointed out to my congregation at the time that there was a counter-image to these two images of interracial violence and hatred. It was the image of Sunday morning in our parish church, where quite literally people of every race and tribe and nation knelt side by side and ate from the same dish and drank from the same cup. Something is lost, however necessary it may be for some people in some circumstances, when it is not visually plain that we eat from the same dish and drink from the same cup, and thus share the Body and Blood of Christ with each other.

The minister distributing communion is directed to accompany the act of placing the elements into the hands of the communicants with words that are designed to focus the communicant on the meaning of the act of communion.

The bread is really and spiritually, in that special sacramental mode of his presence that the Lord has bequeathed to his church, the Body of Christ. The cup is really and spiritually and sacramentally his Blood. The Body and Blood of the crucified, risen, and glorified Lord are indeed the bread of heaven and the cup of salvation. We take them in faith that we might be nourished by the life of Christ and kept in everlasting life. The choice of words is careful here. Apart from God, alienated from God, we are cut off from the source of life. Reconciled to God in Christ, we have a new life with God and with each other, which begins now and which the grave cannot hold. It is the abundant and eternal life that Jesus says, in St. John's Gospel, that he has come to give us. We shall have it in fullness in the end, in the life of the world to come, but we are initiated into this life in our baptism and are nurtured in it and fed by it in our life together in Christ. It is to be renewed in this eternal life, to be kept in it, that we come week by week to the Eucharist.

Although there are a few places in the prayer book that instruct the minister to use a person's name (for instance, in baptism or burial), the instructions for words for delivering the Body and Blood do not include a communicant's name. In the Holy Communion the focus is not on the communicant's relationship with the minister (grateful as communicants are for the presence of the Eucharistic ministers). In this holy and profound moment, the focus is on Jesus and the new life we are being given. Communicants and ministers alike can be at ease, confident that the Good Shepherd does know every person by name.

After receiving Communion, wait for the next person to receive, and then return to your seat. You may kneel or sit quietly in prayer, so that your own worship and that of others is not disturbed. Quiet music is sometimes played during this time of reflecting on the gift just received.

When the distribution of Communion is complete, the unconsumed consecrated elements are gathered up. Either they are reverently consumed by the priest and assisting ministers then and there, or they are reverently set aside to be consumed later. At times there may be such a great quantity left over that it is impractical to consume it all. In this case, the consecrated elements can be dug into the soil. Some parish sacristies have a sink with a drain, called a piscina, which goes directly to the ground so that leftover consecrated wine can be disposed of reverently.

In many places, some of the consecrated bread and wine are set aside for Communion for the sick and shut-ins who cannot be present at the feast. It is a very power-ful symbol of our fellowship with the sick and the shut-in, that they are members with us of the one Body, when the Communion kits for home Communion are filled with the consecrated bread and wine from the parish celebration and taken directly from the altar to the shut-in by the deacon or other appointed persons. Lay persons may be trained and commissioned for this ministry, although historically it is the special ministry of the deacons. In some parishes, a por-tion of the leftover elements will be reserved in a tabernacle or aumbry so that the sacrament is quickly available for ministry to the sick or if additional elements are needed for the distribution of Communion.

The process of dealing with the leftover elements and rinsing out the Communion vessels is called the ablutions. Sometimes the whole process is carried out in the sight of the congregation and sometimes everything is removed to the sacristy or the room where the vestments and vessels are stored and prepared, to be dealt with after the service. Both approaches are entirely appropriate. If the ablutions are likely to be complicated and lengthy, removing the vessels to the sacristy to be taken care of after the service is to be preferred. I like to see all of the vessels removed from the altar, either to a side table or to the sacristy, so that the altar is bare, to signal a shift in our attention, as we come to the post-Communion prayer (page 365).

12

The Sending

DURING THE first part of the service, we kept company with those two disciples on the road to Emmaus as Jesus opened the scriptures to them. During that first part of the service, the Service of the Word, our attention has been on the presence of Christ to us in the Word of God read and preached. During the second part of the service, we kept company with the two disciples as they sat with Jesus at table in Emmaus and he was known to them in the breaking of the bread. Our attention has been on the reality of the Body of Christ in the Eucharistic elements. Now that we have received the Body and Blood of the Lord sacramentally through the Holy Communion, our attention is not on the presence of Christ in the Book or at the table but on his presence in his people gathered who have been renewed in their identity as the Body of Christ by this most holy meal.

So now we pray the post-Communion prayer (page 365). We thank God for accepting us as members of His Son, for feeding us with spiritual food, and we pray to be sent into the world as agents of his peace and love.

Two post-Communion prayers are given in the 1979 Book of Common Prayer. The sentiment in both is very similar. The language of the second prayer is more reminiscent of the first prayer books.

After the prayer a blessing may be given (page 366). The traditional prayer book blessing is "Now may the peace of God, which passes all understanding, keep your hearts and minds in the knowledge and love of God, and of his son Jesus Christ our Lord; and the blessing of God Almighty, the Father, the Son, and the Holy Spirit, be with you now and forever." The congregation responds "Amen"—May it be so!

The Prayer Book catechism, the outline of the Christian faith in the 1979 BCP, says on page 856 that the ministry of the priest includes blessing and declaring pardon in the name of God. There are moments in the service when the priest acts in the person of the people. These are times when the priest gives voice to the common prayer of the congregation—for instance, when the priest asks that the Holy Spirit would act to make the bread and the wine the Body and Blood of Christ for the faithful. At other times, the priest in the Communion service speaks in the person of Christ—for instance, when the priest recites the words that the Savior said over the bread and the wine on the night in which he was betrayed. In the post-Communion blessing, the bishop if present or the priest speaks in the name of God the blessing of God. Recall the first blessing. In the book of Genesis, it is recorded that after God made the heavens and the earth and all the living creatures and the man and the woman, God said, "It is good." In Latin it is *benedicta*, literally "to say good." This is where the word benediction comes from and is the source of the English word blessing.

When the crucified and risen Lord appeared to the disciples cowering in that upper room after the Crucifixion, he breathed on them and he blessed them. "My peace I give you, not as the world gives but my peace." In the death and resurrection of the Lord, in the gift of his Spirit to those who come to him in faith, there is a new Creation. The human race that has fallen into sin and death is being recreated in Christ, and the words of the Father "It is good" are once again able to be heard.

After the blessing, there is usually a post-communion hymn, and then the deacon, or the priest if no deacon is present, gives the dismissal. "Let us go in peace to love and serve the Lord," is typical. "Thanks be to God," the people respond. The people of God have gathered together to be nourished and renewed in Christ, and now are sent out into the world to be the salt of the earth, the light to the nations, and the servants of the Savior's love until he shall come once again in glory.